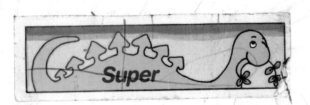

HBJ HEALTH

Green

Consulting Health Educators

Molly Kay Berger, R.N.
School Nurse / Health Educator
Houston Independent School District
Houston, Texas

Carolyn C. Burton
Formerly Coordinator of Student Teaching
 in Health and Physical Education
The University of Texas at Austin

Marianne Litzman
Science Curriculum Coordinator
Calhoun School
New York, New York

Kathleen Middleton
Director of Curriculum
National Center for Health Education
San Francisco, California

Cynthia Olivera
Movement Specialist and Physical
 Education Teacher
Bank Street School for Children
New York, New York

Judith K. Scheer
Formerly Associate Professor
Department of Health Education
The University of Toledo
Toledo, Ohio

Joel B. Shapiro
Teacher of Elementary School Health
 and Physical Education
Community School District 10
Bronx, New York

Nancy L. Young
Teacher and Classroom Supervising Teacher
 for Student Teachers
Royerton Elementary School
Muncie, Indiana

Consulting Health Specialists

Leora Andrew, M.D., F.A.A.P.
Assistant Professor of Pediatrics
Baylor College of Medicine
Section of Child Development
Houston, Texas

Janice Gilyard-Robinson, R.N.
Assistant Professor and
 Pediatric Nurse Specialist
School of Nursing
The University of North Carolina
 at Greensboro

Steven Hutt, D.D.S., F.A.G.D.

David E. Lipson, M.D.
Active Attending Staff
Valley Hospital
Ridgewood, New Jersey

Michael J. Thorpy, M.D.
Montefiore Medical Center
Bronx, New York

Ellen Zaltzberg, R.N.
Health Educator / Nurse
New York City Technical College
Brooklyn, New York

HBJ HARCOURT BRACE JOVANOVICH, PUBLISHERS
Orlando   New York   Chicago   San Diego   Atlanta   Dallas

Editorial Development: Keller/McClanahan, Inc.,
under the supervision of the HBJ Health
Editorial Department
Art Direction and Production Management:
Bookmakers, Inc.

PHOTOGRAPH ACKNOWLEDGMENTS

KEY: T, Top; B, Bottom; L, Left; C, Center; R, Right.

HBJ PHOTOS by Victoria Beller-Smith: 5, 7L, 7R, 8L, 8R, 9,
13, 15, 16, 25, 28, 30, 31L, 31R, 33, 40, 41, 42, 43, 44, 51,
52, 53, 54, 55, 56, 57, 58, 59, 60, 63L, 63R, 73, 81, 83, 91L,
91R, 99, 101, 102L, 103, 104, 106, 109, 110, 111, 113, 114,
115, 119, 125, 126, 128, 130, 132, 137, 139, 140L, 169, 170,
171, 174, 178, 179, 180, 184L, 184R, 185, 194, 200, 205,
207, 211.

HBJ PHOTOS by Frank Crump: 6, 19, 45, 67, 82, 129, 151,
152L, 152R, 156, 158, 160, 161, 162, 172, 176T, 176B, 187.

HBJ PHOTOS by Rob Downey: 11, 77, 107, 135, 148, 163,
175, 201, 206L, 206R.

HBJ PHOTOS by Alan Fontaine: 74TL, 74TR, 75BL, 75BC,
75BR, 84, 85, 86, 87, 88, 90, 93, 138T, 138B, 147, 150, 154,
157, 183, 196, 198.

COVER CREDIT

Focus on Sports, Inc. © David Lissy.

RESEARCH CREDITS: Peter Arnold, Inc., © Barbara Pfeffer:
3. Photo Researchers, Inc., © Larry Mulvehill: 4. Victoria
Beller-Smith: 10, 12, 14, 26. IREX Medical Systems: 38.
Victoria Beller-Smith: 39TL, 39TR, 39BL, 39BR, 61L, 61R.
American Dental Association: 62T, 62B, 65TL, 65TR, 65BL,
65BR, 66T, 66C, 66B. AgroNautics, Inc., Geoffrey Drury: 78.
Victoria Beller-Smith: 79L, 79R. U.S. Food and Drug
Administration: 89. Victoria Beller-Smith: 100. American
Alliance for Health, Physical Education, Recreation and
Dance: 105. Victoria Beller-Smith: 108, 111, 112. Courtesy of
"A Dance Class," Westport, CT: 111. Courtesy of Toshiko
d'Elia: 116L, 116R. Victoria Beller-Smith: 117, 118. Peter
Arnold, Inc., © Manfred Kage: 127. Victoria Beller-Smith:
131, 133, 140R. Taurus Photos, © Alec Duncan: 149.
Courtesy of Ed Cornell: 153. Connecticut Poison Center:
155. U.S. Food and Drug Administration: 159. G.M. Assembly
Division, Public Relations, Warren, Michigan: 173. Courtesy
of Sue August: 177. Victoria Beller-Smith: 181. Monkmeyer
Press Photo Service, © George Zimbel: 182. Victoria
Beller-Smith: 193, 195, 199, 202. National Audubon Society,
© Lincoln Nutting: 203. Photo Researchers, Inc., ©
Porterfield-Chickering: 204. Victoria Beller-Smith: 208.
Courtesy of Elaine Valois: 209. Victoria Beller-Smith: 210.

ART ACKNOWLEDGMENTS

Bob Dole: 32. © Neil Hardy: 29, 34, 36, 37, 64, 92, 102C.
David Moretti: 19, 45, 67, 141, 187. Jan Palmer: 35. Mary
Phenix: 82, 151, 156. Susan Swan: 76. George Ulrich: 186.
All Focus On, Health Career, Health Today, and Beyond the
Classroom border graphics: Thomas Anjiras. Exercise
Handbook: Sylvia Giblin: 217, 218, 219, 220, 222, 223.

CONTENTS

CHAPTER 1

You and Other People

People in families can help one another to be healthy. Friends can help one another to be healthy, too.

The way you act with other people can affect how they feel. The way other people act toward you can affect how you feel. You can learn ways to act with other people that can help you get along with them.

YOUR FAMILY

Think about the people at home. They are members of your **family.** You and the people at home make up your family.

A family can help its members to be healthy. One way a family does this is to help one another feel good. This is called **caring.** Families care by providing food and a place to live. They can show caring in other ways, too.

to take care

Showing Caring

Tricia is practicing her part for the school play. Her family is helping. Her brother, Jeff, is holding a paper with the words Tricia must say. Sometimes Tricia forgets a word. Jeff tells Tricia the word she forgot. Tricia's grandfather calls her a good actress. Her mother says so, too. Tricia smiles. Her family has helped her to feel good. They are showing that they care about one another.

Talking About Ways to Show Caring

How can members of a family show that they care about one another? Talk about your ideas in class.

How are the people in this family showing that they care about one another?

Showing Love

How is Tyrone showing love for his grandmother? How is she showing her love for him?

Tyrone asks his grandmother if she can guess what he has behind his back. Tyrone always has questions for his grandmother. Some of them are hard to answer. She tries to answer every question, anyway. Tyrone's grandmother loves Tyrone very much. Tyrone gives his grandmother the placemat he has made for her. She gives Tyrone a big hug. Tyrone has found one way to show his grandmother that he loves her, too.

Everyone in a family needs love. It can feel good to let other people in your family know about the warm feelings you have toward them.

REVIEW IT NOW

1. What is caring?
2. In what two ways did Tyrone's grandmother show her love to Tyrone?
3. What does everyone in a family need?

FAMILY JOB CHART

	MON.	TUES.	WED.	THURS.	FRI.	SAT.	SUN.
WATER PLANTS		DEBBIE					
FEED FISH		DEBBIE			SAM		DEBBIE
SET/CLEAN TABLE	DAD	MOM	SAM	DEBBIE	DAD	MOM	SAM
WASH/DRY CLOTHES	MOM			DAD			
FOLD LAUNDRY	SAM			DEBBIE			
CLEAN UP LIVING ROOM	DEBBIE	SAM	MOM	DAD	DEBBIE	SAM	DAD
DO DISHES	DAD	DEBBIE	SAM	MOM	DAD	SAM	DEBBIE
WALK DOG	SAM	MOM	DEBBIE	DAD	SAM	DEBBIE	MOM

Look at the Family Job Chart. Do you think Debbie and Sam should trade chores sometimes? Why?

YOUR FAMILY AND YOU

Your family shows caring by helping you in many ways. You can show others in your family that you care about them. One way is by helping your family to work well together.

Doing Your Part

Debbie has just looked at the Family Job Chart. Today is Tuesday. Yesterday, Debbie dusted the furniture in the living room. Her brother, Sam, sorted and folded the clean laundry and walked Pookie, their dog. Today, Sam will vacuum the living-room rug. Debbie has two special things to do. First, she will water all the kitchen plants. Then she will feed the tropical fish. She knows they are hungry. Debbie will do these jobs before she goes to school. Debbie and Sam are helping to do their parts in their family.

Family Physician

Physicians, or medical doctors, check people to make sure they are in good health. They can recognize illnesses and tell when you are sick. Physicians can tell you what to do to feel better and can give you medicine. A *family physician* is trained to treat everyone in a family. A tiny baby and its grandfather might go to the same family physician.

A family physician first goes to college for four years. Next comes four years of medical school. Then, there are one to three years of special training. To learn more about being a family physician, write to the American Academy of Family Physicians, 1740 West 92nd Street, Kansas City, MO 64114.

Health Career

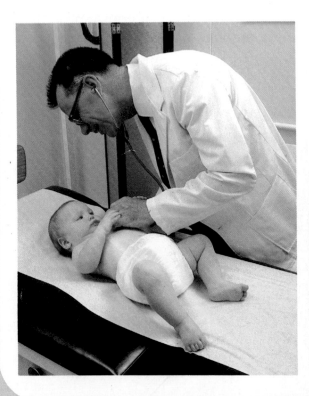
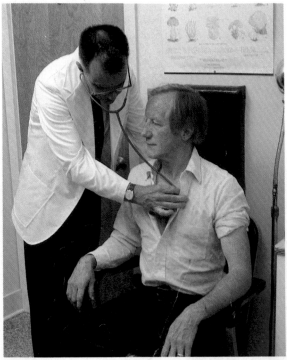

Talking About Being on Time

How might family members help one another by being on time? Talk about it with a classmate.

Peter has just taken a shower. Some water has dripped on the floor. He is using a sponge to soak up the water. Peter puts his dirty clothing in the hamper before leaving the bathroom.

Rosa and Tina Delgado try to be ready when they are called to meals. When a meal is over, Rosa washes the dishes and Tina dries them. Mrs. Delgado thinks her children are a great help.

Peter, Rosa, and Tina do their part to make things work well in their families. They show **cooperation.** They also think about other people's feelings. They show **consideration** for others.

There are things you can do to show cooperation and consideration in your home. Are there special times for eating? Do you do your homework at a certain time? Is there a special time to get ready for bed? Doing things on time will help your family work well. Doing regular jobs around your house helps your family. Picking up your toys and clothing can help your family to work well, too.

What is Peter doing to show consideration for his family? How are Rosa and Tina helping their family?

Paul shared his kite with Wendy. What are some things that are good to share? What might not be good to share?

Getting Along

Paul is Wendy's brother. "What's the matter?" he asks his sister, who looks sad. Wendy has just been asked to be in a kite race in the park. She can't be in the race because she doesn't have a kite. Paul tells Wendy she can use his kite.

When people use the same things, they are **sharing.** Sharing gives people a chance to use things they may not have. Sharing can feel good.

You may not want to share all your things. You may feel that some things are special and are just for you. Brothers and sisters can tell one another which things can be shared.

When Wendy returned the kite to Paul, it was broken. Wendy felt terrible. Paul was angry. She ran to her room. By the time Wendy came out of her room, Paul had fixed the kite. She and Paul talked. Even though it was an accident, they both felt bad about what had happened. In a few hours, they forgot about the accident. Talking helped. So did the passing of time.

Thinking About Needing Understanding

Think about a time when someone your age needed understanding. What was done for him or her? Adults need understanding, too.

Tony and Bill were playing together. Tony tickled Bill. Bill laughed at first. Then he asked Tony to stop. Tony kept tickling Bill. Bill gave Tony a hard push. All at once, the boys were fighting. Later, they weren't sure how the fight had started.

Tony had been teasing Bill. Teasing is doing something to bother someone. Sometimes teasing is making fun of someone. Teasing can sometimes make people feel bad.

People get along better when they try to show **understanding.** To show understanding means to try to know what someone else is feeling. How could Tony have been more understanding?

Gary decided to make corn bread. The directions said to add milk, an egg, and stir. But Gary added too much milk. The mixture was too thin. Gary felt like throwing it away. His sister, Lois, walked in and saw his face. She told Gary she knew how he must feel. Lois showed Gary that she had understanding.

How might these boys be showing understanding toward each other?

REVIEW IT NOW

1. How can you show consideration?
2. What is sharing?
3. What is understanding?

Having a Family Council

What can a family do when two of its members do not agree with each other? The family can have a *family council.* Perhaps a brother and sister do not agree about who owns a book. The whole family sits down together. Each child gets to share with the others his or her opinion about the problem. The brother gives his opinion. The sister gives hers. Then, all the members tell how they see the problem. Finally, the parents help the other members of the family council decide how best to solve the problem.

Not every problem can be solved in a family council. But all members get to talk about their thoughts and feelings. The family council can often be a help in understanding many problems.

Health Today

Thinking About Friends

Think about a good friend. What are three things you really like about that person? What are three things you think that person really likes about you?

Might these children be friends? How can you tell?

Friends are people you like to be with. You may make friends with people in school. You may make friends with people who live near you. Sometimes, you may have one special friend you want to be with.

Anna and Sherry both have puppies. The girls like to get together and play with their pets. You can have fun playing with just one special friend.

Anna likes to play soccer after school. It is fun with a lot of players. So Anna and many friends play soccer in Anna's yard. Sometimes you can enjoy playing with more than one friend at a time.

How Do Friends Act Toward Each Other?

How friends **act,** or the way that they do something, makes a difference.

Sometimes friends just talk to each other. Ricky told Ben about losing his new baseball glove. Ben listened. He knew how bad Ben was feeling. Soon Ricky was feeling better. It is good to have a friend who will listen to you. It is good to be a friend who will listen, too.

Friends can tell each other things that will make each person feel good. Laura liked Tanya's shirt. She told Tanya so. Laura made Tanya feel good.

Friends can also do things that make each other feel jealous or angry or hurt. Jesse showed his new pen to George. Bobby felt jealous. He thought Jesse should show it to him first.

Ira and Chris were playing a game together. Chris grabbed the playing piece Ira wanted. Ira pulled the playing piece out of Chris's hand. Chris didn't want to play any longer.

What are some things that these boys could do to help each other enjoy the game?

Thinking About Problems

Think about a problem two friends could have. How might the problem be solved? Talk over your idea with a classmate. See if the classmate has another idea about what could have been done.

13

How might these friends feel toward each other? How can you tell?

How Can You Get Along with Friends?

It is important for you to know how you are feeling toward a friend. It is also important to decide how to act with a friend. If you are upset with someone, how can you feel better? What can you do to get along with your friend?

Bobby told his mother how he felt. His mother listened to him. Sometimes talking to someone is all you have to do to feel better.

Ira and Chris decided to start their game again. This time, they took turns in their game. Friends can learn to cooperate when they play together. They can make rules that are fair for everyone.

Your friends have feelings just as you do. It is important to know that the way you act makes your friends feel certain ways. Friends can make each other feel good or bad. Try to act in ways that will make your friends feel good.

REVIEW IT NOW

1. What is a friend?
2. What are different ways you can feel with a friend?
3. What are two things you can do if you aren't getting along with a friend?

OTHER PEOPLE

Your family and friends are the people you know best. But they are not the only people you know. Think about all the people you spend time with in a day, or in a week. Even if you are with someone for only a minute, your **actions,** or the things that you do, can be important. Your actions can make you and other people feel good or bad.

How can you know how to act with other people? You can ask yourself, "How do I like people to act toward me? What makes me feel good?" The answers to these questions can help you to know how to act toward other people.

At School

You spend a lot of time with people in school. Getting along with them is important.

Johnny listens when someone is talking to the class. He knows that he wants people to listen to him.

Marie sees how hard the people in the lunchroom work. She thanks them when she gets her food. When she is finished eating, Marie throws away her garbage. Marie's actions show that she is thinking about other people's feelings.

How do Marie's actions show she is thinking of others?

How You Treat People

The way you treat people can make them feel good or bad. When you make people feel bad, they may not treat you the way you would like to be treated. Then you may feel bad, too. When you make people feel good, they may treat you the way you would like. Then you will feel good.

How is Brendan helping Frank feel good?

Frank and Brendan aren't special friends. But one day, Frank came to school with a sling on his arm, which he had hurt. Brendan knew that he would want help if he were Frank. So Brendan helped Frank get his pencil and his books out of his desk. He turned on the water fountain for Frank at recess. He helped Frank in other ways, too. Brendan had put himself in Frank's place.

Mickey took a book back to the school library on time. He told the librarian how much he had enjoyed reading it. The librarian was happy to hear Mickey say that. She had told Mickey the book was one he would like to read. Now, she felt good to know that she had given Mickey the right advice. Telling someone something that makes her or him feel good helps people to get along.

Gerald Salmon

Every week eighteen young people look forward to seeing Gerald Salmon. Gerald is a foster grandparent. There are about 18,000 people in the Foster Grandparent Program. They work in schools, hospitals, prisons, and homes across the country.

Gerald's foster grandchildren are young people who need special help. Most don't have adults in their own families who have the time to guide them. Gerald talks with them. He tells them how important it is to learn as much as they can. Gerald helps his foster grandchildren with their schoolwork. He eats lunch with them every day they are together.

The foster grandchildren help Gerald, too. They make him feel good and useful. Gerald Salmon is one foster grandparent who is making a difference.

Focus On

Marcy helped Mrs. Wilson. How might you help someone today?

Away from School

Many times you meet people away from school. Getting along with them is important.

Angela and Janie were taken to the bus stop. Angela made sure she had the right change. The driver smiled at her. Janie didn't think about change until she was on the bus. The people behind Janie had to wait while she fished in her pockets for the fare. How do you think they felt?

Marcy went to the pet shop to buy a parakeet. At the shop, she saw bags of pet food that had just been delivered. She helped Mrs. Wilson, the shop owner, carry the bags inside.

REVIEW IT NOW

1. What is something you could do today in your school to help someone feel good?
2. What are some things you can do to help people get along with one another?

Charting Chores

Do you do chores at home? People often do many jobs that help the entire family. Think about the chores you do. How often do you do them? What other jobs could you do to help?

Look at the chart below. It shows the chores that Jody did in one week. Every time he finished a chore, he checked it on the chart.

Make a chart similar to Jody's. Write in the chores you could do at home. When you complete a chore, check it on the chart. At the end of the week, read your chart. Are you helping enough at home? How might you help more? Talk about it at home.

Beyond the Classroom

JODY'S CHORES

	MON.	TUES.	WED.	THURS.	FRI.	SAT.	SUN.
SET TABLE	✓						
CLEAR TABLE		✓					
CLEAN ROOM	✓	✓		✓		✓	✓
TAKE OUT TRASH			✓		✓		
WASH DISHES							
DRY DISHES	✓	✓	✓	✓		✓	
WALK DOG					✓		

To Help You Review

Checking Your Understanding

Write the numbers from 1 to 9 on your paper. After each number, write the answer to the question. Page numbers in ( ) tell you where to look in the chapter if you need help.

1. What is a family? (**4**)
2. What is one way family members can show that they care about one another? (**4**)
3. What is one thing that everyone in a family needs? (**5**)
4. What are two ways a family member can help a family work well together? (**8**)
5. What are two good reasons for sharing? (**9**)
6. What are two reasons why teasing may make it hard for people to get along? (**10**)
7. What are friends? (**12**)
8. What are some different ways a friend can make you feel? (**13**)
9. Why are your actions toward other people important? (**15**)

Checking Your Health Vocabulary

Write the numbers from 1 to 8 on your paper. After each number, write the letter of the meaning for the word. Page numbers in ( ) tell you where to look in the chapter if you need help.

1. family (**4**)
2. caring (**4**)
3. cooperation (**8**)
4. consideration (**8**)
5. sharing (**9**)
6. understanding (**10**)
7. act (**13**)
8. actions (**15**)

a. knowing what someone is feeling
b. things that you do
c. you and the people at home
d. people using the same things
e. helping others to feel good
f. the way that you do something
g. thinking about other people's feelings
h. helping one another to make things work well

Each of the words below tells about a person or people. Write the numbers from 9 to 13 on your paper. After each number, write a sentence using each word.

9. family
10. friends
11. sisters
12. brothers
13. grandparents

Practice Test

True or False?

Write the numbers from 1 to 15 on your paper. After each number write *T* if the sentence is *true*. Write *F* if it is *false*. Rewrite each false sentence to make it true.

1. Family members always have the same feelings about one another.
2. A family can help its members to be healthy.
3. Family members can make one another feel good.
4. If you do not do things on time, your family can work well together without you.
5. Winning at a game is an example of showing consideration for others.
6. You must share everything you have.
7. Teasing can mean making fun of someone.
8. Teasing never bothers anyone.
9. No one can understand how other people feel.
10. It is always better to play with only one friend at a time.
11. Just listening to a friend's troubles can be helpful to the friend.
12. Following rules in a board game is a way to cooperate.
13. When you have a bad feeling, it may help if you tell someone about it.
14. Your actions can show that you are thinking about other people's feelings.
15. The way you act can make your friends feel bad or good.

Complete the Sentence

Write the numbers from 16 to 20 on your paper. After each number, copy the sentence and fill in the missing word.

16. People can work well together when they show _____ with one another.
17. Your _____ are people you like to be with.
18. Trying to know how someone else is feeling shows _____ .
19. You can feel good by _____ some of the same things with people.
20. Your _____ is made up of you and the people at home.

Learning More

For You to Do

1. Look into your mirror to see how others see you. Imagine that you feel angry. Study your face in the mirror. Now, imagine you have just enjoyed a good time with a special friend. Study your face again. Notice how your face shows your feelings to other people.

2. Choose a close friend. Talk about these ideas with your friend:
   - When did you first meet?
   - On first meeting, what did you like about each other?
   - Have there been some things you did not agree on? How did you settle your differences?

For You to Find Out

1. Talk to an adult in your family. Find out more about the childhood of this person. Ask questions such as these: How many brothers and sisters lived with you? What things did you share with them? Who were your closest friends? What things did you do with these people? Are you still friends with any of them?

2. Answer each riddle below. You will be using words like "aunt," "grandmother," "uncle." You may wish to work with a friend to decide the answers.
   - Which person is your mother's father?
   - Who is your father's mother?
   - What would your father's brother be to you?
   - Who is your mother's child?

For You to Read

Here are some books you can look for in your school or public library. They can help you find out more about getting along with other people.

Naylor, Phyllis Reynolds. *Getting Along with Your Friends.* Abingdon, 1980.

Viorst, Judith. *Alexander and the Terrible, Horrible, No Good, Very Good Day.* Atheneum, 1975.

CHAPTER 2

You Are Growing

You have been growing for a long time. You have changed a lot over the years. You can see some of these changes. They have to do with the way you look and act. But many changes take place inside, where you can't see them. Some of these changes have to do with your body, too. Others have to do with your thoughts and feelings.

Your growing-up years are exciting ones. And it is exciting to know that you can have something to do with the way you grow. If you follow good health practices, you will help yourself grow in the very best way you can.

What are some things that this baby needs her parents to do for her?

GROWING

Some of your greatest growing has already taken place. You will grow a lot more.

Your First Year

Babies are different **weights** when they are born. Your weight is how heavy you are. Eric was 6 pounds (about 2½ kilograms). Jenny was 9 pounds (about 4 kilograms). But babies grow all the time. At the end of his first year, Eric weighed 20 pounds (about 9 kilograms). Jenny weighed only a little more. By the age of one year, a baby may have grown up to three times its weight at birth.

Newborn babies can't help themselves. Someone has to feed them and keep them warm and dry. Someone has to give them love. Newborn babies can't even hold up their heads by themselves. Someone else has to hold up their heads, turn them over, and move them from one place to another.

Babies begin learning right away. They learn by seeing, hearing, and tasting. They learn by touching, moving, and making sounds. Babies also learn to **trust.** When the same people help a baby all the time, the baby learns to trust them. The baby feels they will always be there when the baby needs them.

Jenny saw and touched her parents' faces many times every day. Jenny's parents always smiled and talked softly to Jenny. When Jenny was around five months old, she began to smile back at them. Jenny was learning to know and to trust her mother and father. When babies trust other people, they can feel safe. Feeling safe helps them grow in a healthy way.

Every baby grows at its own rate. During her first year, Jenny made a lot of sounds. So did Eric. Both babies listened to other people, too. At the end of her first year, Jenny could say a few words. Eric didn't begin to talk until he was about 15 months old.

Pretending You Are a Baby

Pretend you are a baby lying on your back in your crib. What are some things you might see, hear, taste, and touch? Draw pictures of some of these things.

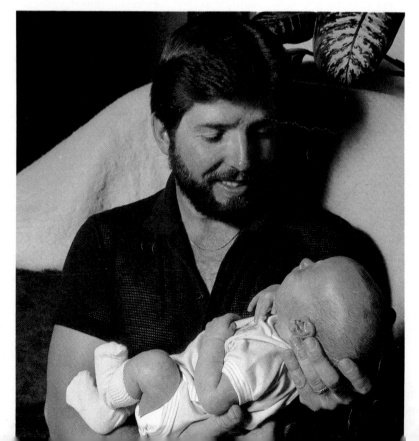

How might Eric be feeling? How can you tell?

Looking at Younger Children

Do you know any three-, four-, or five-year-olds? What are some things they can do now that they couldn't do when they were babies? Share your findings with your classmates.

Eric and Jenny moved around more and more as time went on. By the time she was a year old, Jenny could crawl around the house. She could see where everything was. She could also see that things had more than one side. This made Jenny feel happy. At Eric's first birthday party, he could walk around, holding onto things. Eric felt very proud of himself. Eric's parents were proud, too.

Before you can move around, you can only see things close to you. After you know how to get around by yourself, you can discover other things.

Getting to Where You Are Now

Children keep on growing and learning. Children learn to use words to say what they want. They learn to use their bodies to do new things, such as running, climbing, and balancing. They learn more about the world around them. They learn to do more things for themselves. Each child keeps growing and learning in his or her own way. All children do not learn the same things at the same time. Each child is different.

How does this picture show that children keep growing and learning in their own ways?

Sandy has just gotten a bigger bicycle. Her old one was too small. It used to seem so big. But Sandy's legs began to bump into the handlebars when she pedaled.

Sandy is changing in other ways, too. Her face is not as round as it was last year. She also has some big, new teeth in the front of her mouth.

Sandy's new teeth are **permanent teeth.** These are the second set of teeth. The first set of teeth is called **primary teeth.** Primary teeth begin to come in when a baby is about six months old.

As you grow, your permanent teeth slowly form under the others. They will push out the primary teeth. Your permanent teeth are the last set of teeth your body will grow.

As you grow, your body becomes ready to do more things. You are able to learn more **skills.** These are things you are able to do well. With some skills, you use your hands and eyes together. These are called eye-hand skills. Raul wrote to his last year's teacher, Mrs. Grasso. She told Raul his writing was much better than it used to be. Raul's eye-hand skills had improved.

With some skills, you use your whole body. Janie began hitting balls with a bat this year. She seemed to know just when to hit and how to swing the bat.

Children may learn skills at different times. Max has been swimming since he was a baby. Betty learned how to swim after her sixth birthday.

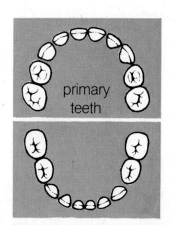
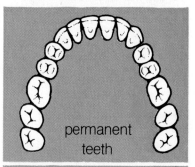
primary teeth

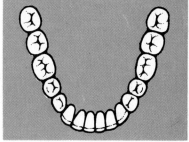
permanent teeth

Why might you find a primary tooth next to a permanent tooth?

What skills might John be learning while he plays checkers with his grandfather?

Children don't all learn the same skills. John doesn't play ball very often. But he likes to play checkers with his grandfather. Fran loves to stand on her head and to do cartwheels.

As you grow, you can do more things for yourself. You make more **choices.** A choice is something you decide for yourself. Wes knows he must do his homework every day. But he can help choose when he will do it. As you grow, you will get to decide more and more things for yourself.

REVIEW IT NOW

1. What are some things a baby may learn during its first year?
2. What are your two sets of teeth called?
3. What are some things children your age can do now that they could not do when they were younger?

Sealing Teeth in Plastic

Now dentists can really help children protect their permanent teeth. Dentists can seal permanent teeth in plastic. First, the dentist cleans the tooth. Then, he or she paints the tooth with a special liquid. The liquid helps hold the plastic onto the tooth. A special light hardens the plastic. The plastic coating helps prevent tooth decay. It also makes the biting and grinding surfaces of the teeth extra strong.

The dentist usually starts with the molars (back teeth) that come in when children are about six years old. The dentist can also paint adults' teeth to protect them. Dentists are trying to make tooth decay a thing of the past!

Health Today

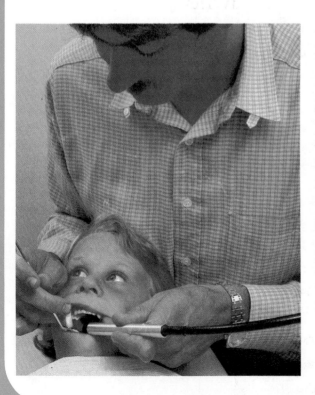
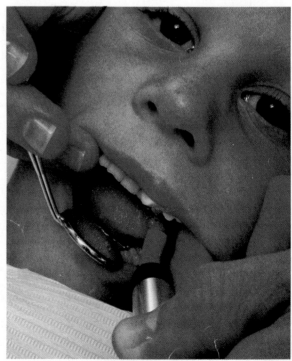

GROWING YOU CAN SEE

There are ways to tell whether you have grown. But you cannot see this growth day by day.

Getting Taller and Heavier

A scale can show you what your exact weight is. You can weigh yourself on a home scale. You can also get weighed in the doctor's or the school nurse's office. The scales that the doctor and nurse use give you the most exact weight. Some scales may have rulers on them. The ruler on a scale measures your exact **height,** or how tall you are.

You can find out for yourself how tall you are by using a yardstick or a tape measure. You can also stand against the wall and have someone mark the

What does a scale tell about the way in which you are growing?

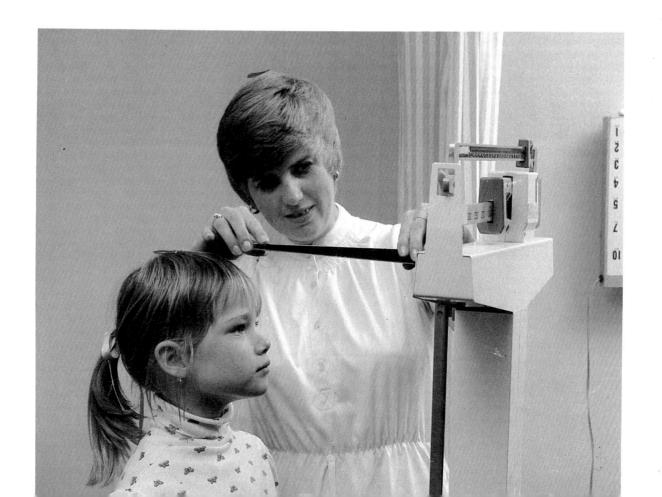

How can you tell that Donald is growing?

wall behind your head. Be sure to put a piece of tape on the wall first. If you measure yourself in the same way and place every few months, you will have your own record of how much you have grown.

Outgrowing Your Clothes

Donald outgrows his shoes every year. This fall, Donald couldn't wear some of the clothes that fit him last spring. Some of Donald's shirts and pants were too tight. Some of the sleeves and legs were short. All this means that Donald's arms, feet, and legs have grown. He may have gotten bigger across his chest, waist, and hips, too. Children outgrow their clothes because they are slowly getting taller and heavier. They are growing!

REVIEW IT NOW

1. What are three different ways you can tell that growth has taken place?
2. What are the two most exact ways to find out your height and weight?

Inside Your Cells

Each of your cells has a thin wall around it. Materials from the food you eat pass through this wall. Wastes also leave the cell through this wall. Inside each cell is a watery material like jelly. In the middle of each cell there is a dark spot called the **nucleus.** The nucleus directs the activities of the cell. It is the most important part of every cell.

Different parts of your body grow at different rates. Your hands and feet grow faster than your arms and legs. This growth happens so slowly that you can't see it. Some of your growing takes place inside your body. You *cannot* see it happen, either.

Your Cells

Cathy's teacher said our bodies are made up of billions of **cells.** Cells are the smallest living parts of our bodies. Most of the cells in our bodies are making new cells all the time. This is how we grow.

Our skin is made up of one kind of cell. Other parts of our bodies are made up of other kinds of cells.

Cathy stared at her skin. She tried to see her cells. Her teacher said that cells are too tiny to be seen in that way. We can see cells only through a **microscope.** A microscope can make very small things look bigger.

Could you see a cell by just looking at your skin? Why?

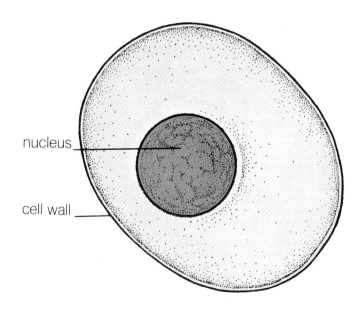

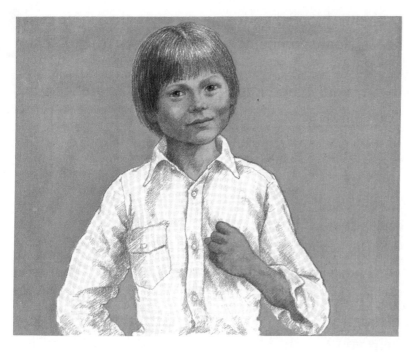

Will this boy's heart always be the same size? Why?

Your Heart

Put your hand toward the left side of your chest. You can feel your **heart** pumping, or beating. Your heart is inside your chest. It is a thick, hollow muscle that pumps blood all around your body. Your heart pumps all the time.

Close your hand and make a fist. Your heart is about the size of your fist. Your heart is still growing. It will reach its full size by the time you are in your early teens.

When your heart beats, it is squeezing its walls together. Then some blood squirts out into big tubes. The blood leaves your heart through these tubes. They are called **blood vessels.** Blood is carried around your body through smaller blood vessels. Blood is carried back to your heart through blood vessels, too. Between beats, your heart rests, and blood comes back into it.

Your Blood Vessels

There are more than 10,000 miles (16,000 kilometers) of blood vessels in your body. Stretched out, they would go halfway around the world.

Your blood has materials in it that your body needs. Some come into your blood from the food you eat. Some come from the air you breathe. The part of the air your blood needs is **oxygen.** Oxygen is a gas you cannot see, taste, or smell.

Your Lungs

Put your hand under your nose. Can you feel the air as it goes out? First you feel it, then you don't. That is because you are breathing by pulling air into your nose and letting it out the same way. When you breathe in, the air goes down your throat and through your windpipe into your **lungs.** Your lungs help you breathe.

Your body needs the oxygen from the air. When you fill your lungs with air, the oxygen goes into air sacs in your lungs. Your blood carries the oxygen to cells in all the other parts of your body. The oxygen

Where does air enter your body? Where does it go after it leaves your windpipe?

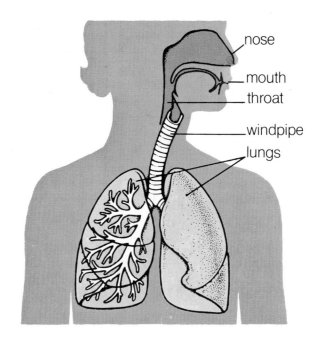

36

helps turn food into **energy.** Energy is the strength your body uses to do its work.

As you grow, your lungs grow. So they are always able to hold as much air as your body needs.

Your Brain

Put your hands on the top of your head. Under those hard bones is your **brain.** Your brain is used to think. It also tells your body when to move and to do other things. Your brain is growing. You cannot see it growing.

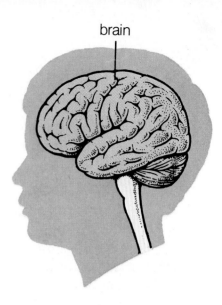

brain

In what ways does your brain control your body?

Your brain receives messages from all parts of your body. Then it tells your body what to do. Nancy was crossing the street when she heard a siren. She quickly ran back to the curb. Nancy's ears sent a message to her brain. Her brain then sent a message to her legs, and she moved to the sidewalk.

Your brain controls your seeing, tasting, and smelling. It also controls your breathing, your heartbeat, and many of your body's other activities. It controls your feelings, too.

Do you remember what you ate for lunch yesterday? Your brain will remind you. Your brain is the place where you keep information. Your brain is what makes you able to read this book.

REVIEW IT NOW

1. What are cells?
2. What carries blood through your body?
3. Why does your body need oxygen?
4. What are some of the things your brain does?

Sonographer

Did you know that sound can be used to see inside your body? A *sonographer* uses a sonogram machine to do just that. The sonogram machine sends sound through the body. The sound echoes back and makes a picture on a special screen. Sonographers can take pictures of the heart, liver, eyes, and other parts of the body.

After high school, sonographers take special training programs lasting two to four years. To learn more about being a sonographer, write to the American Registry for Medical Diagnostic Sonographers, 2810 Burnet Avenue, Cincinnati, OH 45219.

Health Career

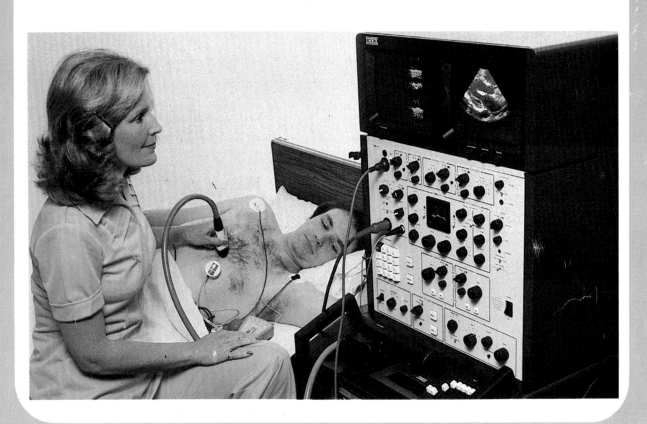

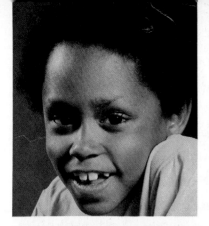

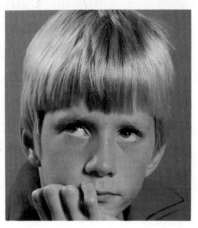

What is the same about all these faces? What are some differences?

GROWING IN YOUR OWN WAY

You probably know many children your age. Not one of them is just like you. None of them thinks and feels just like you do. None of them acts just like you do. None of them looks just like you do, either. You are special. They are special, too.

One thing about you that is special is the way your face looks. Another thing is the color of your hair and your eyes.

Your size and shape are special, too. Your size means how much you weigh and how tall you are. Children your age are many different sizes.

Your shape may come from how much you weigh. It may also come from the size and shape of your bones. Children your age are many different shapes and sizes.

Tracing Your Body

Would you like to get a good idea of your shape? Get a big sheet of paper. Stretch it out smoothly on the floor. Lie down flat on the paper. Have someone trace your outline with a crayon. Write your name on the back. Look at the shapes made by everyone. Guess whose shape is whose.

Susie and Lynne are exactly the same age. They used to wear some of each other's clothing for fun. Susie tried on Lynne's new blouse. This time, Susie's hands didn't even reach the bottom of the sleeves. Susie and Lynne aren't the same size anymore. Both girls are growing. But each girl is growing in her own way.

Lynne may be growing faster than Susie. Susie may catch up later. Or Lynne may grow into a taller adult than Susie. It is too soon to tell. Everyone's way of growing is different.

When many children are nine or ten, they begin to grow very fast. Other children grow slowly until they are older than that. There is no one right way to grow.

Some girls may keep on growing taller until they are about 18 years old. Some boys may keep growing even longer. When you reach your full height, you may get heavier. But you will not grow any taller.

These boys are both the same age. How do they show that everyone's way of growing is different?

Dolores Laurice

Eight hundred children depend on Dolores Laurice each summer day. Dolores is a nurse at a day camp in New Jersey. She believes that children must have good health care.

Every five to ten minutes a camper visits Dolores. She treats everything from cuts to insect bites. She gives ear drops and takes temperatures. She also keeps medicines that some campers' parents ask her to give. Dolores has a refrigerator filled with yogurt and apple juice to help campers swallow certain medicine.

During the rest of the year, Dolores is a school nurse. She enjoys helping children and seeing them grow throughout the year.

Focus On

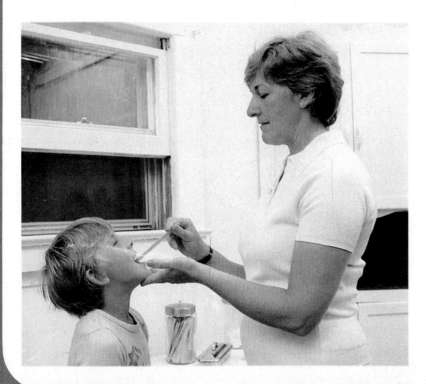

Listing Family Traits

In what ways do members of your family look alike? Make a list of the physical traits your family members share.

A **trait** is a feature that tells something about you. A **physical trait** is a feature that tells something special about your body. As you grow, the way you will look may have something to do with the way your parents look. Members of a family share some physical traits.

Mrs. Gartler and her daughter have some of the same physical traits. Mrs. Gartler came to pick up Linda after Ellen Stern's birthday party. Mrs. Stern opened the door and said, "You must be Linda's mother. You look just like her." Linda and her mother both have very fair skin. They have gray eyes and dimples in their chins, too.

In Mike's family, Mike, his sister, and his brother all have red hair. In Julie's family, she and her brother both have long, dark eyelashes.

What physical traits do the people in this family share?

Children with one or two tall parents may grow up to be tall like their parents. Children with heavy parents may gain weight more easily than children whose parents are thin. You have many special physical traits. Some of these traits have been passed on to you by your parents and their parents.

What physical traits do the people in this family share?

Helping Yourself Grow

There are things you can do to help yourself grow in a healthy way. Nelson Porter wants to help himself grow as he should. He has done many things today that will help him grow.

First, Nelson ate a healthful breakfast. He had foods that would give him energy and help him grow as he should. Then he rode around on his bike all morning. Nelson sat quietly and read before lunch. After lunch, he played kickball with his friends. Before his next meal, he went into his room and sorted his shell collection. Then he ate a healthful dinner.

How is Nelson helping himself grow in a healthy way?

After dinner, Nelson noticed a few red spots on his arm. He knew that some of his friends were ill. Nelson showed the spots to his mother. Mrs. Porter said the spots were just mosquito bites. She told him there was nothing to worry about. So Nelson played checkers with his sister until bedtime. He was in bed in time to get a good night's sleep.

You can help yourself to grow by following these rules every day:

1. Eat healthful foods.
2. Get exercise.
3. Get plenty of rest and sleep.
4. Report any signs that you may be ill to an adult.

REVIEW IT NOW

1. In what three ways do children your age look different from one another?
2. What is a physical trait?
3. How can you help yourself grow as you should?

Making a Family Measurement Chart

You have been growing in size since birth. You will keep growing until you are between 18 and 20 years old. You will get taller and gain weight. Your head, neck, wrists, hands, and feet will get bigger, too.

A family measuring chart will often show these facts. Make a chart like the one below. Then use a measuring tape or string and ruler. Take the measurements shown for each person in your own family.

You may take the measurements in inches or centimeters. Look over your chart. What does your information tell you?

Beyond the Classroom

FAMILY MEASUREMENT CHART

	FATHER	DANIEL 8 years old	KIRA 4 years old	MOTHER
DISTANCE AROUND WRIST	7 inches	5 inches	4½ inches	5½ inches
DISTANCE AROUND HEAD	23 inches	21 inches	20 inches	22 inches
DISTANCE AROUND NECK	15½ inches	11 inches	10 inches	12 inches
LENGTH OF FOOT	11 inches	8 inches	7 inches	9 inches
WIDTH OF HAND WHEN FINGERS ARE OPEN	9½ inches	6½ inches	5½ inches	8½ inches

To Help You Review

Checking Your Understanding

Write the numbers from 1 to 15 on your paper. After each number, write the answer to the question. Page numbers in ( ) tell you where to look in the chapter if you need help.

1. About how many times its weight at birth may a one-year-old baby weigh? **(26)**
2. Why is it important for a baby to learn trust? **(27)**
3. What are three things a one-year-old might be able to do? **(27-28)**
4. What are some new things children can do as they grow older? **(28)**
5. What is an example of using your hands and eyes together in practicing a skill? **(29)**
6. What is a skill you use your whole body for? **(29)**
7. What are two exact ways to measure growth? **(33)**
8. Why can't you see a cell without a microscope? **(34)**
9. What happens when your heart beats? **(35)**
10. When you breathe in, where does the air go? **(36)**
11. What does your blood carry that your body needs to turn food into energy? **(36-37)**
12. How does energy help you? **(37)**
13. What are some things your brain does? **(37)**
14. When do girls and boys usually stop growing in height? **(40)**
15. What are some physical traits you can get from your parents? **(42-43)**

Checking Your Health Vocabulary

Write the numbers from 1 to 6 on your paper. After each number, write the letter of the meaning for the word or words. Page numbers in ( ) tell you where to look in the chapter if you need help.

1. weight (**26**)
2. trust (**27**)
3. height (**33**)
4. blood vessels (**35**)
5. oxygen (**36**)
6. energy (**37**)

a. a gas you cannot see, taste, or smell
b. how tall you are when you measure yourself
c. the strength your body uses to do its work
d. tubes that carry blood around your body
e. how heavy you are when you get on a scale
f. feeling people will always be there when they are needed

Write the numbers from 7 to 17 on your paper. Then write a sentence that explains the meaning of each word or words. Page numbers in ( ) tell you where to look in the chapter if you need help.

7. permanent teeth (**29**)
8. primary teeth (**29**)
9. skills (**29**)
10. choices (**30**)
11. cells (**34**)
12. microscope (**34**)
13. heart (**35**)
14. lungs (**36**)
15. brain (**37**)
16. trait (**42**)
17. physical trait (**42**)

Practice Test

True or False?

Write the numbers from 1 to 15 on your paper. After each number, write *T* if the sentence is *true*. Write *F* if it is *false*. Rewrite each false sentence to make it true.

1. Newborn babies may stop growing for many months.
2. Babies begin learning right after they are born.
3. All babies grow and learn at the same rate.
4. Moving around keeps babies from learning.
5. As they grow older, children keep learning new things.
6. You can grow a new tooth whenever one falls out.
7. As you grow, you can make more choices for yourself.
8. You outgrow your clothing because it shrinks in the wash.
9. You get new cells only until you become an adult.
10. Your blood is constantly moving all around your body.
11. When you breathe in, your lungs get bigger.
12. Your brain receives messages from all parts of your body.
13. Your brain controls only your breathing and your heartbeat.
14. All children the same age are the same size and shape.
15. There are things you can do to help yourself grow.

Complete the Sentence

Write the numbers from 16 to 20 on your paper. After each number, copy the sentence and fill in the missing word or words.

16. Your size is how _____ you are and how much you _____ .
17. We grow because our cells make new _____ all the time.
18. Different children may learn different _____ .
19. Children all grow at _____ rates.
20. Children have some of their parents' _____ _____ .

48

Learning More

For You to Do

1. Find photographs of yourself as a baby, a two-year-old, and a five-year-old. Or, ask an adult in your family what you looked like at those ages. Now look at yourself in a mirror. How have you changed at each age? In what ways have you stayed the same?

2. Weigh yourself once a week for a month. Use a scale at school or at home. Keep a record of your weight. See if your weight has changed at the end of the month.

3. Make a list of things you have done in one day to help yourself grow in a healthy way.

For You to Find Out

1. As babies grow, they learn to do more things. Use a library book or an encyclopedia. Find out how old most babies are when they learn to do these things:
   - smile
   - sit up
   - walk

2. Talk with an adult in your family. Find out what size shoe and shirt you wore last year. Then look inside a shoe and a shirt you now wear. Compare the sizes.

For You to Read

Here are some books you can look for in your school or public library. They can help you find out more about your body and how it grows.

Brenner, Barbara. *Bodies*. Dutton, 1973.

Harris, Robie H., and Levy, Elizabeth. *Before You Were Three—How You Began to Walk, Talk, Explore, and Have Feelings.* Delacorte Press, 1977.

McNamara, Louise Greep. *Your Busy Brain*. Boston: Little, Brown, 1973.

CHAPTER 3

Taking Care of Yourself

As you get older, you begin to do more things. You take care of yourself more and more, too. You make choices every day that have to do with being healthy, happy, and safe.

When you keep your hands, face, hair, teeth, and the rest of your body clean, you are doing things to be healthy. Wearing the right clothing helps keep you healthy and comfortable. Giving yourself enough rest and sleep every day also helps you to feel good and to be healthy. Taking care of yourself will help you to stay healthy and to look your best.

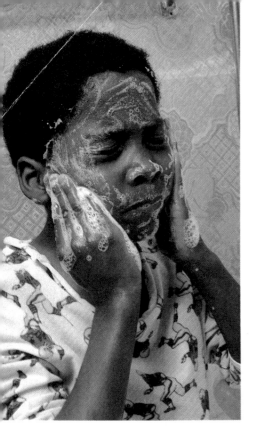

What should this boy do so that his face will not become chapped?

KEEPING CLEAN AND HEALTHY

You are covered by skin from your head to your toes. Your skin helps keep you from becoming ill. Your skin needs special care. Your hair and clothes need care, too.

Washing Your Face and Hands

Each morning and evening, Terry washes her face with warm water and a mild soap. She makes sure to wash every part of her face. Then she carefully rinses and dries her face, so it won't get **chapped.** Chapped skin feels rough and sore.

When Terry washes her face she is removing some oil from her skin. The skin is made up of many layers of cells. The layer you can touch is your **epidermis.** The cells in this top layer are dying all the time. New cells from your **dermis,** or bottom layer, keep replacing the cells that have died.

Inside your skin are about two million **sweat glands.** These glands have tiny tubes that carry sweat out of your body. Sweat is a salty, liquid waste. Your skin has **oil glands,** too. They send out oil that is made in your skin. The oil keeps your skin soft and moist. Both sweat and oil leave your skin through small openings called **pores.**

When You Sweat
Your body is always making heat. You would be too hot if some heat couldn't get out of your body. Some heat leaves your body when you sweat. In the hot sun, your skin sweats a lot. The sweat then dries. As it dries, it cools your skin.

While you're asleep, some oil comes out of your pores. Washing your face every morning removes oil and sweat. It also keeps your pores open. Washing your face at night removes oil, sweat, and dirt.

There is another, very important, reason for washing your face in the evening. Washing carefully removes any **germs** that have gotten on your skin during the day. Germs are tiny living creatures. Germs can be seen only through a microscope. Germs live almost everywhere.

Many germs are helpful. Some germs prepare soil so plants can grow in it. Some help turn milk into cheese. Some germs can be harmful. These germs can make us ill if they get inside our bodies. You can carry germs from your hands to your mouth, your nose, and your eyes. You can carry germs from your hands to a cut in your skin.

Why will these children need to wash their hands when they finish playing?

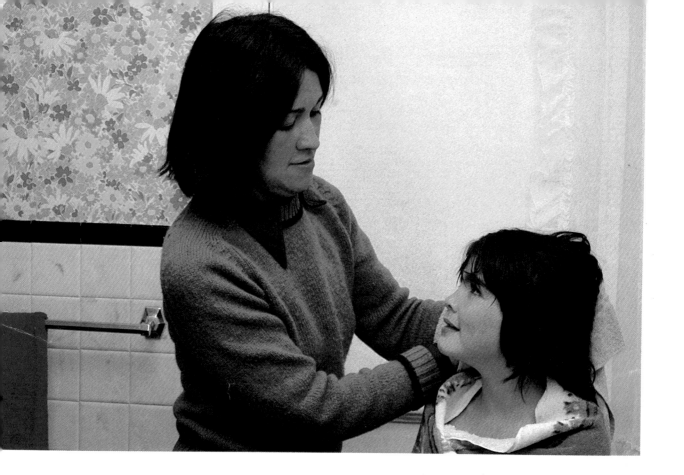

How does bathing help keep your body clean and healthy?

Bathing

Even the parts of your body that are covered by clothes most of the time need to be washed. When your body isn't washed often, germs on your skin may cause odors.

Julius loves taking showers. They make his body feel relaxed. Elyse usually likes baths better. Both are good ways to get clean.

Wash your body with warm water and soap. If water is too hot, it can dry out your skin. If it's too hot, it can also burn your skin. Soaping yourself all over will help loosen the oil and dirt. Be sure to wash small, hard-to-reach spots such as the creases of your skin. Rinsing and drying well are important. It is also important to be very careful not to slip getting in and out of the tub or shower.

Keeping Your Hair Clean

Dirt and germs from the air, and oil from your skin, gather quickly in your hair. Wash your hair as often as necessary to keep it clean.

Even clean hair can have health problems. One such problem is **head lice.** These are tiny insects that can live on the scalp, making it itch. Monica told her grandmother her head itched. Her grandmother looked closely at Monica's scalp. She saw that she had lice. She washed Monica's hair with a special medicine. Then she combed it with a special comb. She also washed Monica's pillowcase and other things that had touched her head. She wanted to stop the lice from going to other people's scalps.

Curly Hair, Straight Hair

Your hair has roots. If your hair roots are round, you will have straight hair. If your hair roots are flatter, you will have curly hair. The shape of your hair roots doesn't change. Is your hair more straight or curly?

Whom did Monica tell when her head began to itch? Why was it important that she told an adult?

Wearing Clean Clothing

By the end of the day, Daniel's clothes have picked up a lot of dirt. Sweat has soaked into his clothing, too. Sweat can make clothing smell bad. Daniel's feet sweat because they are in a closed-in, dark place most of the day. He makes sure he wears clean clothes and clean socks every day.

Caring for Small Cuts and Scrapes

Your skin does a very good job of protecting you. But sometimes you may get a small cut or scrape somewhere on your skin. When your skin is open, dirt and germs can get into your body. Small skin breaks can also sting and throb.

Marlene was playing tag when she fell. Her knee hurt. She saw she had scraped off some skin and gotten dirt in her scrape. When Marlene got home, she did what her parents had taught her to do. First, she washed her knee with warm water and soap to clean out the dirt. Then she dried her knee and put a bandage on it. Later, she showed the scrape to her mother.

If you hurt yourself, you should show the hurt place to an adult. If you have only a small scrape or scratch, you can help yourself until you can show your problem to an adult.

Sometimes you may get a sore place on your skin. Jerry had been wearing gym shoes without socks. The shoes kept rubbing against his heels. His heels began to feel very sore. Jerry had gotten painful blisters on his heels. You should never break blisters. If you do, you will make an opening for germs to enter. But you can make blisters feel better by

Why should Daniel wear clean socks every day?

Small Cuts and Scabs

When you get a small cut, a little skin gets broken. The cut bleeds because small blood vessels are cut at the same time. Soon, the blood hardens and dries. This closes the cut so it won't bleed anymore. A scab forms over the skin. When the cut skin is healed, the scab falls off.

stopping whatever is causing them from rubbing. Putting a bandage over the blister may help, too. Soon, the blisters will go away by themselves.

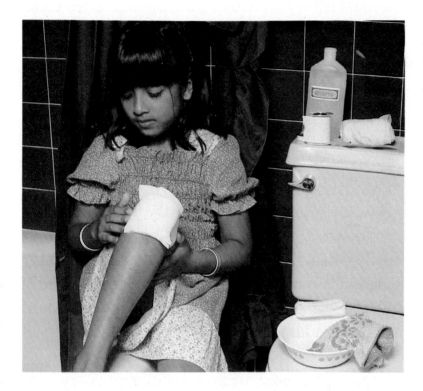

What are three things that should be done to treat a scrape on the skin?

REVIEW IT NOW

1. What two glands are found in your skin?
2. How can germs enter your body?
3. Why is it important to wash your hands more than once a day?
4. What are two things you can do if you get a small cut or scrape?

It was nearly half an hour after Ricky's bedtime. He could hardly keep his eyes open to read his book. He had to put down his book. In a minute he was asleep.

Ricky had worked and played hard all day. His body had used up a lot of energy. So he soon fell asleep. Now his body could build up more energy.

Sleeping

When you sleep, your heartbeat and breathing slow down. Your body can build up a new energy supply while you sleep. Children need more energy than adults because children are growing. So most children your age need more sleep than most adults do. Most children your age need about 11 hours of sleep.

Everyone's need for sleep is different. Your body tells you if you are getting as much sleep as you need.

Joan went to bed late and got up very sleepy. She was almost late for school. She couldn't seem to move fast enough. In class, she didn't notice when Mrs. Miller spoke to her. Joan dropped things and bumped into people all day. She felt so grouchy she didn't even want to play with her friends. Joan knew she needed more sleep than she had gotten.

That night Joan went to sleep early. Her room was quiet with plenty of fresh air. The next morning, Joan woke up feeling full of energy. She knew it would be a good day.

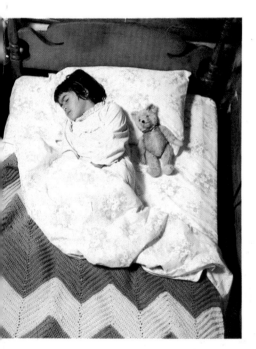

How does sleeping help your body build up new energy?

58

Michael Thorpy

Michael Thorpy is an unusual doctor. He invites people into his hospital laboratory to watch them sleep. Some people have trouble sleeping. Michael studies them carefully. He measures their brain activity patterns. Their eye movements and muscle activity are charted as they sleep. Then Michael can train the people when and how to sleep normally.

Michael Thorpy wants to find out why we need sleep every night instead of every week or month. He is very interested in studying dreaming and how it affects our health. We know that our bodies get tired without sleep. Michael Thorpy is trying to find out exactly how sleep helps keep us healthy.

How are these boys resting?

Resting

There are times during the day when you need to rest. When your body is working hard, the oxygen and food that give your cells energy are being used up. Your body needs a chance to slow down so it can build up new energy.

You can find a way to rest wherever you are. In school, walk instead of run in the schoolyard. At home, find an activity that is relaxing and peaceful. You might lie down and close your eyes for a few minutes.

REVIEW IT NOW

1. Why do most children need more sleep than most adults?
2. About how much sleep do most children your age need every night?
3. Why do you need to rest after being very active?
4. What are two ways you can rest?

Biofeedback

Scientists have found one way that can help some people control their bodies. It is called *biofeedback.* For example, a person can help control his or her own heartbeat if it is too fast. The person is connected to a special machine. If the person's heart is beating too fast, a bell goes off. Then the person can think about slowing his or her heartbeat. After training, the person can slow the heartbeat just by thinking about it.

Scientists are not exactly sure how biofeedback works. They are studying it carefully to understand its uses better. Some people think that someday biofeedback may help children learn better.

Health Today

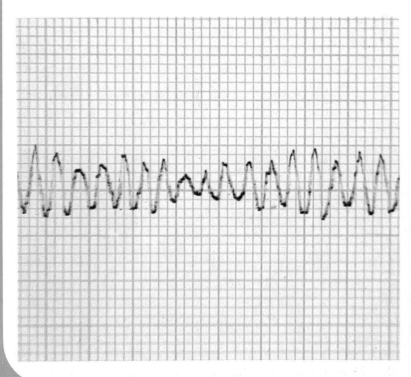

At school, Lea finished her lunch. Then, she went into the girls' bathroom and took some big mouthfuls of water. She sloshed the water around in her mouth. Lea rinsed out any bits of food that might be left over in her mouth after lunch.

Lea's dentist, Dr. Wang, had checked Lea's teeth and gums the day before. She told Lea all the things she should do to keep them in good condition. One was to brush her teeth after every meal. If Lea couldn't always do this, Dr. Wang told her to rinse her mouth after every meal.

Dr. Wang wanted to make sure that Lea removed **plaque** from her teeth. Plaque is a thin, sticky film of germs. It forms on the **enamel,** or hard, outer layer of your teeth. Usually you can't see plaque. Sometimes you can feel it with your tongue. Dr. Wang gave Lea a tablet called a **disclosing tablet.** It has a harmless red dye in it. When Lea chewed the tablet, parts of her teeth appeared red. The red parts showed where Lea's teeth had plaque on them.

What does the red dye in a disclosing tablet show on teeth? How does using a disclosing tablet help people?

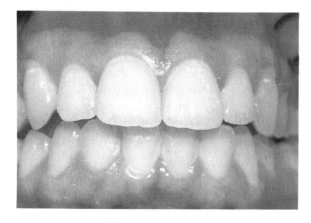

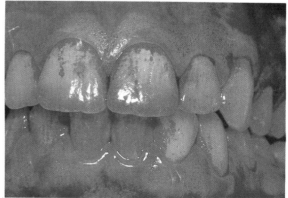

Dentist

For healthy teeth and gums, regular checkups by a *dentist* are important. Dentists can help prevent tooth decay. They can repair holes in teeth if they do form. Dentists can also make teeth appear more beautiful. They can replace lost teeth. Dentists teach their patients the best ways to care for their teeth and gums.

Most dentists complete four years of college. Then, they complete four years of dental school. Many dentists take one or two years of extra training, too. To learn more about being a dentist, write to American Dental Association, 211 East Chicago Avenue, Chicago, IL 60611.

Health Career

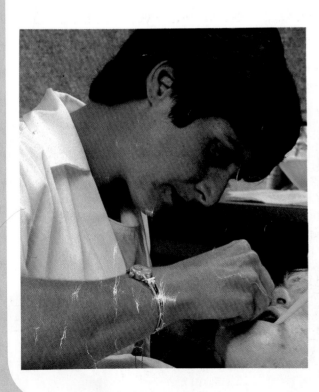

How Tooth Decay Happens

Plaque causes **cavities,** or tooth decay. It can also harm your gums. Dr. Wang cleaned Lea's teeth. When she was done, all the red dye was gone. Dr. Wang also checked Lea's mouth for any sign of tooth decay. She found no signs of trouble.

How do you get cavities? When you eat foods that have sugar in them, the germs in plaque make **acids.** Acids are chemicals that usually have a sour taste. Eat healthful foods. Avoid foods with a lot of sugar. They are strong enough to break down tooth enamel. After a time, too much acid can make a hole in the enamel. A hole in the tooth enamel is called a cavity. If the cavity isn't fixed, it gets bigger and deeper. Then a hole can form in the next layer of your tooth, the **dentin.** If the cavity gets worse, the inside part of your tooth, the **pulp,** can begin to decay, too. A cavity can kill your tooth.

You need a good, strong set of teeth so you can chew your food. Teeth also help give shape to your face. Healthy teeth and gums are part of good health.

enamel
dentin
pulp
gum
bone
places where cavities can form

How are cavities formed? What can you do to avoid them?

Brushing Your Teeth

One of the best ways to remove food and plaque from your teeth is to brush them every day. Brushing after each meal is best. If you cannot, try to rinse your mouth out after every meal. Then brush the first chance you get.

Many toothpastes contain a chemical called **fluoride.** Fluoride helps protect your teeth against tooth decay. Use it if your dentist tells you to. Visit your dentist as often as he or she tells you to.

These pictures show one method of brushing.

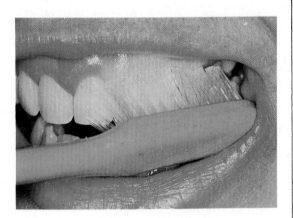

Steps 1 and 2

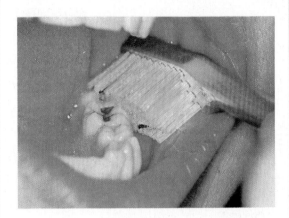

Step 3

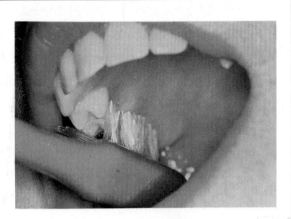

Steps 4 and 5

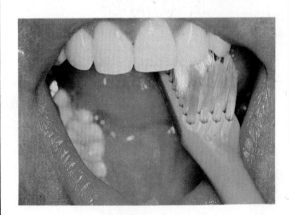

Step 6

1. Tilt your brush against your teeth where your teeth and gums meet.

2. Gently move the brush back and forth many times. Use short strokes.

3. Brush the outside of your upper and lower teeth and your gums.

4. Brush the inner part of your upper and lower teeth and your gums.

5. Brush the chewing surfaces of all your teeth.

6. Brush the inside of your front teeth. Hold the brush straight up and down. Make several up and down strokes with the front end of the brush over your teeth and gums.

7. Gently brush your tongue.

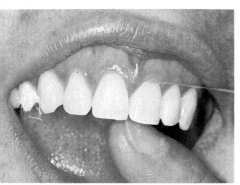

Another good way to remove plaque and bits of food from between your teeth is to use **dental floss.** Dental floss is a strong white thread used to clean under your gums and between your teeth. Try to floss your teeth before you go to bed each night.

Some people think flossing is difficult. It is easy with practice. Ask an adult for help. These directions and pictures will help.

1. Break off a piece of dental floss about 18 inches (75 centimeters) long.
2. Wind most of the floss around the middle finger of one hand. Wind the rest around the middle finger of the other hand.
3. Hold about an inch (2½ centimeters) of the floss tightly between your thumbs and your forefingers.
4. Gently move the floss back and forth between two teeth. When you reach your gum, curve the floss against a tooth.
5. Move the floss away from your gum by moving it against the side of your tooth.
6. Do the same thing for all of your teeth.

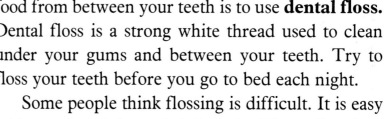

What areas does dental floss reach that a toothbrush might not?

REVIEW IT NOW

1. Why is plaque harmful to teeth?
2. Why is sugar harmful to teeth?
3. Why is it important to brush and floss your teeth?

Graphing Your Own Sleep Patterns

Some children need 12 hours of sleep a night. Others feel refreshed after only 8 hours of sleep. Do you know how many hours of sleep you usually get? Try this activity. For one week, write the time you go to bed each night. Write the time you wake up each morning. Figure out how many hours of sleep you had. Make a graph like the one below. Each morning, color in a bar on the graph to show how many hours you slept. At the end of the week, study your graph. How much sleep do you usually get? Are there nights you sleep fewer hours than you do other nights? How do you feel when you wake up in the morning? After how many hours of sleep do you feel your best?

Beyond the Classroom

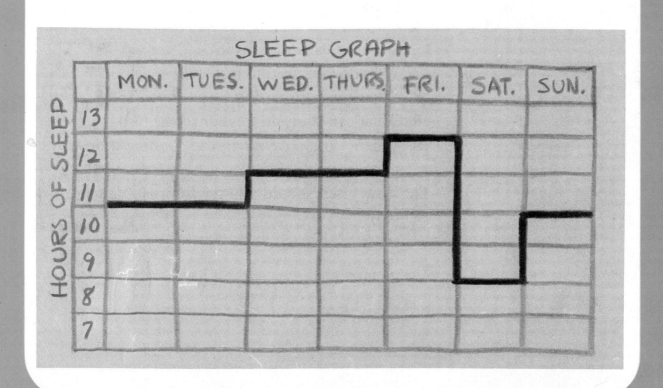

SLEEP GRAPH

To Help You Review

Checking Your Understanding

Write the numbers from 1 to 11 on your paper. After each number, write the answer to the question. Page numbers in ( ) tell you where to look in the chapter if you need help.

1. What are four things that washing removes from your skin? (**52–53**)
2. What are four ways that germs can enter your body? (**53**)
3. Which is best for your skin—hot, cold, or warm water? (**54**)
4. What are head lice? (**55**)
5. How can you help yourself if you have a blister on your foot? (**57**)
6. How many hours of sleep do most children your age need each night? (**58**)
7. Why do you need to rest? (**60**)
8. What can a disclosing tablet show? (**62**)
9. What can acids do to your teeth? (**64**)
10. Where does a cavity spread to after it destroys tooth enamel? (**64**)
11. How often should you try to brush your teeth? (**64**)

Checking Your Health Vocabulary

Write the numbers from 1 to 6 on your paper. After each number, write the letter of the meaning for the word. Page numbers in ( ) tell you where to look in the chapter if you need help.

1. pores (**52**) **4.** enamel (**62**)
2. germs (**53**) **5.** acids (**64**)
3. plaque (**62**) **6.** pulp (**64**)

a. inside part of a tooth
b. small openings in your skin
c. hard, outer layer of a tooth
d. tiny, living creatures
e. thin, sticky film on teeth
f. chemicals that usually taste sour

Write the numbers from 7 to 11 on your paper. Read each sentence and fill in the missing word or words. Page numbers in ( ) tell you where to look in the chapter if you need help.

7. You should always rinse and dry your face well, or it may become _____ . (**52**)

8. Oil is sent out of your skin through tiny tubes called _____ _____ . (**52**)

9. The top layer of your skin is the _____ . (**52**)

10. The bottom layer of your skin is the _____ . (**52**)

11. Take care of your teeth to avoid _____ . (**64**)

12. A chemical called _____ helps protect your teeth against tooth decay. (**64**)

Practice Test

True or False?

Write the numbers from 1 to 15 on your paper. After each number, write *T* if the sentence is *true*. Write *F* if it is *false*. Rewrite each false sentence to make it true.

1. Your skin cleans itself.
2. Germs can enter your body only through a cut.
3. The best way to wash yourself is with soap and cold water.
4. It is a good idea to wear clean clothes every day.
5. Head lice are tiny insects that live on the scalp.
6. It is important not to break blisters.
7. It is best to leave small scrapes and scratches alone.
8. Some nights, you don't need sleep.
9. Resting helps your body build up new energy.
10. Enamel, dentin, and pulp are all parts of your gums.
11. Plaque is caused by disclosing tablets.
12. Eating too much sugar can help cause tooth decay.
13. You should try to brush your teeth after every meal.
14. It is a good idea to gently brush your tongue when you brush your teeth.
15. You only need to floss your front teeth.

Complete the Sentence

Write the numbers from 16 to 20 on your paper. After each number, copy the sentence and fill in the missing word or words.

16. Washing your face every morning helps keep your _____ open.
17. Skin that is _____ feels rough and sore.
18. When you have a cut or scrape, _____ may enter your body through your skin.
19. When you sleep, your body doesn't use as much _____ as when you are awake.
20. It is important to use _____ _____ to clean under your gums and between your teeth.

70

Learning More

For You to Do

1. Remember to visit your dentist for checkups. While you're there, talk with the dentist. Ask how the different tools and machines are used to help keep your teeth healthy.

2. The next time you lose a primary tooth, look at it carefully. Does it have any cavities that you can see? Does it have a filling? Compare it with a permanent tooth in your mouth. How is it the same? How is it different?

3. Ask an adult in your family to help you set up a *first-aid kit*. A first-aid kit is a container with the things you need in case someone gets a cut or scrape. An empty shoe box makes a good container. Try to include clean pieces of cloth to wash the cut or scrape. Also include some bandages of different sizes and a medicine to kill germs on the skin. Discuss with your family where it would be best to keep the kit. The kitchen or bathroom are two good choices.

For You to Find Out

1. How does soap work to clean your body? What is it made from? How is it made? Use an encyclopedia to find the answers.

2. Why doesn't it hurt when you cut your nails or hair? Use a library book or an encyclopedia to find the answer.

For You to Read

Here are some books you can look for in your school or public library. They can help you find out more about taking good care of yourself.

Rockwell, Harlow. *My Dentist.* Greenwillow, 1975.

Showers, Paul. *Sleep Is for Everyone.* Crowell, 1974.

Wolf, Bernard. *Michael and the Dentist.* Four Winds, 1980.

CHAPTER 4

Food and Food Choices

Most people like to eat. You probably have your favorite foods. You may enjoy eating certain foods with your family or your friends.

Your body must have different kinds of food every day. It needs food so it can do its work. Your body needs food so it can make energy. Your body needs energy to grow.

Eating healthful food helps you to feel good and to be healthy. It is important to learn all you can about eating healthful food.

FOOD ALL AROUND YOU

You depend on plants and animals for the food you eat. Some foods you eat come from plants. Some foods come from animals.

Food from Plants and Animals

You eat parts of plants all the time. Usually, you eat just one part of a plant. When you eat carrots and beets, you are eating the roots of plants. Potatoes are underground stems. Asparagus is the main stem of a plant. Celery is the stem and leaf of another plant. Spinach, lettuce, and cabbage are the leaves of plants. Broccoli and cauliflower are the flower buds.

What parts of plants are shown on these pages?

broccoli

lettuce

When you eat an apple, you are eating a plant's fruit. The fruit is the part that holds a plant's seeds. Pears, grapes, plums, and bananas are also fruits. Tomatoes, cucumbers, and green peppers are fruits, too. What else do you eat that has seeds inside?

Sometimes you eat the seeds of plants. Peanuts, lima beans, and nuts are seeds. Grains such as rice, wheat, and corn are also seeds that you can eat. Perhaps you have eaten pumpkin seeds or sesame seeds.

Many of the foods you eat come from animals. Different parts of animals can be eaten. For example, meat from cows, sheep, pigs, chickens, and fish can be eaten.

From Seeds to Bread

People all over the world eat bread. There are many kinds of bread—brown and white, heavy and light, soft and hard. All bread is made from flour. Flour is made from grain, which is the seeds from certain plants. Grain is one of the most important parts of the world's food supply.

asparagus

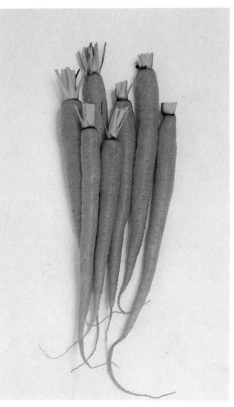

carrots

pumpkin seeds

Often you can tell by looking at meats which animal they come from. But sometimes it is hard to know. The meat from an animal may be cut into small pieces or chopped up. It may also be mixed with other foods before it is served.

Animals also make certain foods for us. We get eggs from chickens. Milk comes from cows. We make cheese and certain other foods from the milk that cows give us.

From which animals do the foods shown here come?

The Food Chain

The plants and animals we eat are part of the **food chain.** People are also part of the food chain. The term *food chain* means that plants, animals, and people are linked in an important way.

The food chain begins with green plants. Green plants make their own food. To do this, they use sunlight, air, and water from the soil. Animals can't make their own food. So they eat plants and other animals. People can't make their own food, either. They eat plants and animals, too. Dead animals and plants feed the soil. This also helps green plants to grow. Plants, animals, and people all use one another to stay alive.

What do these plants need to make their own food?

REVIEW IT NOW

1. What are six parts of plants we can eat?
2. What foods besides meat can we get from animals?
3. What part of the food chain makes its own food?

Hydroponics

One way of adding to our food supply is to use *hydroponics.* Hydroponics is a way of growing plants without soil. For example, tomato plants usually grow in soil outdoors. Using hydroponics, farmers put the roots of tomato plants in water, sand, or gravel. They add plant food. They also pump oxygen into the water. They make sure the plants get enough warmth and light, too.

Raised this way, plants can grow indoors. Many plants, such as tomatoes and lettuce, can grow in warm greenhouses during the middle of a snowy winter. Hydroponics can also be useful in places with dry soil or no soil at all.

WHY YOU EAT FOOD

Melanie asked her mother to put some extra fruit and nuts in her lunchbox. Her mother knows Melanie is eating more because she is growing.

Your Body Needs Energy

The food you eat gives your body **nutrients.** These are parts of food that help your body grow and give you energy. Energy is the heat that food gives you when the food in your body is burned. It is the oxygen in your blood that burns the food and turns it into energy. You need energy to work and play and study. The nutrients in food give you the energy you need.

Which children are using more energy? How can you tell?

We can measure the amount of energy nutrients give our bodies. Energy is measured in **calories.** A calorie tells you how much energy the food you eat gives your body when the food is burned.

Different foods have different amounts of calories. A tablespoon (14 grams) of peanut butter has about 95 calories. A stalk of celery has about 5. Getting enough calories will give your body energy. Some people get more calories than their bodies need. When this happens, their bodies turn the extra calories into fat. If your body is carrying too much fat, you may not be as healthy or as comfortable as you might be.

You Enjoy Eating

You also eat because you enjoy it. Becky and her friend Yvette went to Becky's house after school. They felt hungry. Becky found apples in the refrigerator. She picked the two reddest ones and washed them. She gave one to Yvette. The apples felt cold on the girls' tongues. They tasted sweet and juicy. They were crunchy, too. Apples are fun to eat. They are also a healthful food.

Your favorite foods are the ones that taste best to you. Sometimes, you want to taste food because of how it smells or the way it looks. The way food feels in your mouth is also a reason why you enjoy eating it.

Part of the fun of eating is being with other people. In many families, certain times are set aside as mealtimes. Eating at these times may become a **habit.** A habit is something you do often without thinking very much about it.

You Eat What Your Family Eats

What you and your family eat depends on many things. Most families care about how much foods cost. People often try to buy foods that are on sale. Joey and his aunt went shopping. They saw the big SALE sign over the chicken. Joey's aunt bought two packages, one to eat that night, and one to freeze for another time.

Some families may eat certain foods because of their food tastes. Some families have special beliefs. These beliefs may affect their **diet.** A diet is what a person usually eats and drinks.

Arnold likes to try many new foods. Nita likes to eat foods that she is used to. Both Arnold's and Nita's families eat turkey at Thanksgiving. Many families have special meals that they eat on special holidays.

Many families enjoy eating foods that come from other countries. Often, these foods have been served in their families as far back as anyone can remember.

Looking Up Foods of the World

Some restaurants serve foods that are most often found in other countries. Check the Yellow Pages of your telephone book. Look under the heading "Restaurants." How many kinds of food from other countries can you find? What are the names of those countries?

What are some reasons why people may eat certain foods?

What is the main ingredient in this food? Why might this food not be very good for you?

You See Foods Advertised

People sometimes eat certain foods because of advertisements they see on TV and in magazines. Advertisements can make food look delicious. The people who make the advertisements want you to buy the food you see.

Food that is made to look good may not always be very good for you. Some soft drinks have a lot of sugar in them. Too much sugar can be harmful to your teeth and heart. Sometimes you might fill up on food that your body can't use. Then, you may not want to eat food that your body needs.

It is important to think about the food you eat. Think about the **ingredients,** or things that go into a food. Many foods are put into packages. You can find the ingredients of these foods listed on their packages. The first ingredient listed is the main one in the food. An adult can help you check labels. You can decide to avoid foods that aren't good for you.

REVIEW IT NOW

1. What are nutrients?
2. With what do we measure energy?
3. What is a diet?
4. What are ingredients?

FOOD GROUPS AND HEALTHFUL FOOD CHOICES

What is this girl going to drink? Why is this nutrient important?

Foods can be put into four different groups. Each group contains many different nutrients. Different nutrients do different jobs. Some foods have nutrients that give you energy right away. Nutrients in some foods give you energy you can store. Some foods give you nutrients that help you grow.

Water is a very important nutrient. You need water to stay alive. Water is in and around your cells. It carries other nutrients to all your cells. You get water from most foods you eat. There is also water in milk and juices. But you should still drink a few glasses of plain water every day.

No one food supplies all the nutrients your body needs. You need a **balanced diet.** This means you should eat food from each of the four food groups every day. They are shown on the next four pages.

FRUIT AND VEGETABLE GROUP

BREAD AND CEREAL GROUP

MILK GROUP

MEAT GROUP

How will the foods Sherry ate help her grow in a healthy way?

Eating a Balanced Diet

The longest time your body goes without food is between your evening meal and your breakfast. By breakfast time, your body needs the energy that a good breakfast can give it.

Look at the pictures of meals on this page. Look at what Sherry ate for breakfast today. From which food groups did her breakfast come? Now look at the rest of Sherry's meals. Did she eat a balanced diet today? A balanced diet should also include plenty of water.

Food and Drug Administration Inspector

Food and Drug Administration Inspectors protect all of us. They make sure that food, drugs, and cosmetics are safe. They visit food manufacturers to check that the food labels are correct. The factories must be clean. And they may not have insects or mice.

To become a Food and Drug Administration Inspector, you need four years of college, with courses in science or home economics. Then you get on-the-job training during the first year of work. To learn more about being a Food and Drug Administration Inspector, write to the Food and Drug Administration, 5600 Fishers Lane, Rockville, MD 20857.

Health Career

Not all food you eat may be eaten at meals. You may eat some snacks during the day. If you decide to eat snacks, choose foods from the four food groups.

You can have fun mixing different foods for snacks. Sometimes Mike has slices of apple and cheese with fruit juice. Joey loves yogurt with peaches. Linda eats raw carrots with peanut butter. All the foods you see on this page make tasty and healthful snacks.

Why are these snacks healthful? What are ways you could combine these foods to make healthful snacks?

Erick Swanson

When Erick Swanson goes fishing, he catches just what he wants. Erick runs a fish hatchery in Connecticut. He raises trout from eggs. Fish are very healthful food. By raising fish, Erick helps to increase the food supply. He sells thousands of fish each year.

Erick starts with thousands of trout eggs in a small tank. As the fish hatch, he feeds them carefully. He also pumps oxygen into the water and keeps the water warm. After 12 months, Erick has large tanks full of adult-size trout. Then he dips nets into the tanks and chooses the fish he wants to sell. Erick enjoys running the hatchery and helping to feed a lot of people.

Digesting the Food You Eat

Your body turns the food you eat into the energy you need. Your body breaks up the food and changes it so your cells can use it. This is called **digestion.**

The food you swallow goes down a pipe called your **esophagus.** From there, it moves into your **stomach.** In your stomach food is squeezed, mashed, and turned into a thick liquid.

Food stays in your stomach for a few hours. Then it is moved into your **small intestine.** This is a long tube that is curled up inside you so it can fit. Water and other nutrients from the food go into blood vessels in your small intestine. The blood vessels take the nutrients to the cells of your body. The parts of the food your body can't use are called **wastes.** Wastes go into your **large intestine.** After many hours, the wastes can leave your body.

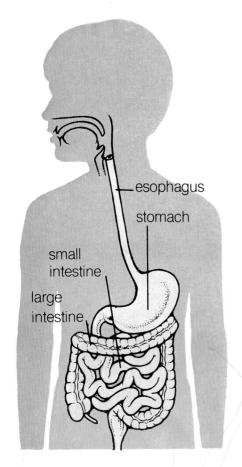

How does digestion change the food you eat into the nutrients your cells need?

esophagus

stomach

small intestine

large intestine

REVIEW IT NOW

1. What are the four food groups?
2. How can you get a balanced diet?
3. What is it called when your body breaks up food and changes it?

Looking Carefully at a TV Ad

Beyond the Classroom

Sometimes food ads on TV are very flashy and fast moving. The ads use colorful pictures and catchy music to sell foods. Look carefully at a TV food ad. Decide for yourself if the ad presents a healthful food. Then ask yourself these questions:

- In which food group does this food belong?
- Might this food have too much sugar? Will this food help balance my diet today?
- Was the ad funny? Was it exciting? Was it beautiful? Would I choose to eat this food? Why or why not? Was it the ad that was actually appealing or the food?

Talk about this ad with an adult at home.

To Help You Review

Checking Your Understanding

Write the numbers from 1 to 12 on your paper. After each number, write the answer to the question. Page numbers in ( ) tell you where to look in the chapter if you need help.

1. What are some foods that come from plants? (74-75)

2. What different foods do we get from animals? (75-76)

3. What are the three parts of the food chain? (77)

4. How do nutrients help your body? (79)

5. What do calories measure? (80)

6. What are four reasons why you might like certain foods? (80)

7. What is a reason why a person might not eat a certain food? (81)

8. Why might certain foods not be good for you? (82)

9. Where can you find information about what ingredients are in a food? (82)

10. Why do you need to eat many different kinds of foods? (83)

11. What are the four food groups? (84-87)

12. What are some healthful snacks? (90)

Checking Your Health Vocabulary

Write the numbers from 1 to 6 on your paper. After each number, write the letter of the meaning for the word or words. Page numbers in ( ) tell you where to look in the chapter if you need help.

1. food chain (**77**)   **4.** ingredients (**82**)

2. nutrients (**79**)   **5.** balanced diet (**83**)

3. calories (**80**)   **6.** digestion (**92**)

a. measure of how much energy food gives the body

b. the linking of plants, animals, and people

c. food from each of the four food groups

d. how your body breaks up and changes food

e. parts of food that help your body grow and give you energy

f. things that go into a food

Write the numbers from 7 to 12 on your paper. Then write a sentence that explains the meaning of each word or words. Page numbers in ( ) tell you where to look in the chapter if you need help.

7. habit (**80**)   **10.** stomach (**92**)

8. diet (**81**)   **11.** small intestine (**92**)

9. esophagus (**92**)   **12.** large intestine (**92**)

Practice Test

True or False?

Write the numbers from 1 to 15 on your paper. After each number, write *T* if the sentence is *true*. Write *F* if it is *false*. Rewrite each false sentence to make it true.

1. We eat many parts of plants.
2. People could live if there were no green plants.
3. We eat only the meat of animals.
4. Food passes from your esophagus to your stomach to your large intestine to your small intestine.
5. Food is squeezed and mashed in your stomach.
6. Your small intestine receives food from your stomach.
7. If you get more calories than you need, you will grow very strong.
8. We like foods only because of their taste.
9. People's beliefs may affect their choice of foods.
10. Most people eat exactly the same kinds of foods.
11. Many families have special foods they like to eat.
12. Food shown in advertisements on TV is always good for you.
13. The four food groups are meat, fish, fruits and vegetables, and soup.
14. Snacks should be healthful for your body.
15. A balanced diet should include water.

Complete the Sentence

Write the numbers from 16 to 20 on your paper. After each number, copy the sentence and fill in the missing words or words.

16. Your body needs _____ from different kinds of foods.
17. Your body turns extra _____ into fat.
18. Eating meals at certain times may become a _____ .
19. You can make sure your daily _____ has the nutrients your body needs.
20. Eat enough foods from each of the four _____ _____ every day.

Learning More

For You to Do

1. Keep a food diary for one whole day. Write down everything you eat and drink. Then study your information. What foods are you eating? Can you make your diet more healthful? How?

2. Look through a cookbook. Find a simple, healthful, interesting recipe. It could be something different from anything you have ever eaten. It might be from a different country. Make the food yourself. Or ask an adult to help you.

3. Look through magazines for pictures of food from the food groups. Design a healthful meal. Cut out the pictures and paste them on a paper plate. Label the plate "A Healthful Meal."

For You to Find Out

1. Some foods give us many products. For example, yogurt and cheese are made from milk. Read some food labels. Find the main ingredient of each of these foods: peanut butter, raisins, popcorn.

2. We eat the leaves, stems, roots, flowers, and seeds of plants. Use a library book or an encyclopedia. Find out which part of these plants we usually eat: radish, corn, lettuce, rhubarb.

For You to Read

Here are some books you can look for in your school or public library. They will help you find out more about foods and healthful food choices.

Aliki. *Green Grass and White Milk*. Crowell, 1974.

Paul, Aileen. *Kids Cooking Without a Stove*. Doubleday, 1975.

CHAPTER 5

Exercising for Fun and Health

You use your body in all kinds of ways. When you run, climb, jump, and stretch, you use your body. You also use your body when you swim, dance, or ride a bicycle.

Being active is fun. It makes you feel good. It is also important for your health. Being active makes your body stronger.

You may enjoy doing some activities more than others. There are many ways to be as active as you need to be. You can try different ways until you find the activities that are best for you.

Recording Your Activities

In what ways did you exercise today? Maybe you climbed some stairs. Perhaps you did some running. How many active things do you think you will do before you go to bed tonight? Make a record of this information.

Alan has worked and played hard today. In the morning, he helped Mr. Wexler carry six gerbil cages downstairs to the pet fair. In gym, Alan ran through an obstacle course. He also did some rope climbing. After school, Alan played softball with his friends.

Alan has used his body in many different ways today. He has gotten a lot of **exercise.** Exercise is any activity that makes your body work hard.

When you get exercise, many parts of your body move more than they usually do. Regular exercise is one of the best ways to have a healthy body. It is also one of the best ways to make yourself feel good.

How are these children helping themselves to have healthy bodies?

Your Muscles and Bones

How do muscles and bones help these children jump rope?

Touch your arm. You can feel your skin. Your skin is one of the **tissues** of your body. Tissues are groups of the same kinds of cells that work together. Now, squeeze your arm. You can feel your **muscles.** Muscles are groups of tissues that help your body move. Exercise is a form of movement.

Muscles are attached to your bones and other parts of your body. For example, certain muscles move your eyes. Other muscles move your body by pulling on your bones. Muscles work in pairs to help your body move. Bend your arm. One muscle pulls your arm bones up. Now, straighten your arm. Another muscle pulls the same bones down.

Muscles and bones work together to help your body move. Bones are another kind of tissue in your body. You have 206 bones. These bones form your **skeleton.** Some parts of your skeleton protect the inside of your body. Your skeleton also helps give your body its shape.

How do your muscles know when you want to move your bones? Your brain sends a message along certain cells to the muscles you want to move. As the muscles get the brain's message, they do their job.

Heidi wants to run around the park twice without stopping. Her leg muscles are working hard. They are burning up a lot of energy as she runs. Her muscles need more energy when she runs than when she is still.

What are this boy's muscles doing to help him ride his bicycle?

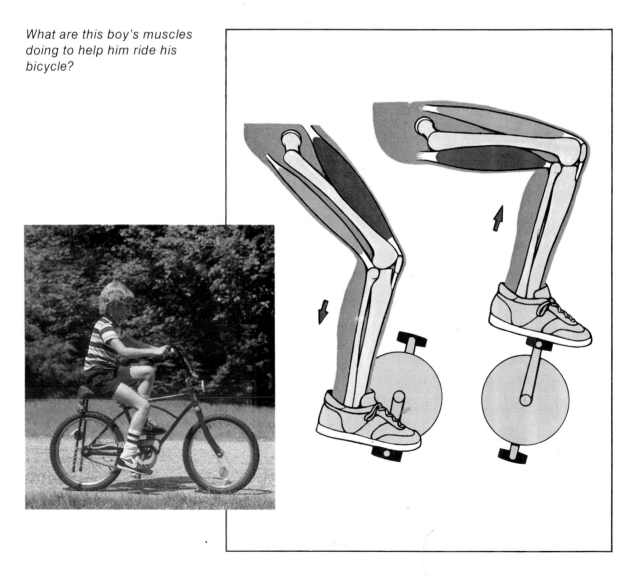

What happens inside Heidi's body when she runs?

When Heidi runs, she breathes deeper and faster. Her lungs are working harder than usual. They are taking in more oxygen to give to her blood. Heidi's body uses more oxygen when she exercises. Heidi's heart is pumping faster. It must send blood with oxygen and nutrients to the muscles in her legs. The nutrients and oxygen give Heidi's muscles the energy they need. Then the blood races back to her heart and lungs. The blood is carrying wastes from the cells. The wastes leave Heidi's body when she breathes out.

REVIEW IT NOW

1. What is exercise?
2. What three parts of your body help your body to move?
3. How does your blood help your body when you exercise?

How does jogging help these people feel stronger and healthier?

WHY EXERCISE?

Everyone in the Marchi family is active. Sonia Marchi runs, climbs, jumps, and stretches. Mr. and Mrs. Marchi jog together early every morning. The Marchi family enjoys exercising.

You Feel Good

Mr. and Mrs. Marchi used to drive everywhere they had to go. They got very little exercise. They often felt tired if they walked even a few blocks.

Now, the Marchis feel stronger and healthier. After they jog in the morning, their bodies are relaxed. The Marchis go through a day with more energy. Exercising helps them feel wide awake, too. When the body gets a good workout, even the brain gets more oxygen.

Talking to People About Exercise

Talk to your family and adult friends who seem to be very active. What do they do to keep in shape? Ask them questions. How long do they exercise? How often do they exercise? Why do they exercise?

Jumping Rope for Health

Did you know that jumping rope can be a very exciting sport? More than one million students take part in *Jump Rope for Heart.* Before the event, teams learn how to jump rope correctly. They also learn the importance of exercising regularly. Students from kindergarten to college join in. They ask people to give a penny or a dime for each minute their team jumps at the event. The students give the money to the American Heart Association.

Special teams show people fancy tricks at *Jump Rope for Heart.* These teams interest others in this healthful sport.

Health Today

In what three ways is exercising helping this boy's muscles?

Your Body Works Better

If you do regular exercise, your body will grow stronger. Your heart will get stronger. It will be able to pump more blood every time it beats. Your lungs will get stronger, too. They will be able to hold more air every time you take a breath.

When you do regular exercise, you can help your muscles in three ways. You can help your muscles to become stronger. You will be able to exercise longer without becoming tired. Your muscles will be able to move more easily.

Barbara wanted to jump high over a rope. She practiced a lot. Every few days, she raised the rope. Her leg muscles had to work hard. The daily exercise made them stronger and stronger. Barbara's leg muscles got firmer. Firmness of muscles is called **muscle tone.** After a few weeks, Barbara could jump much higher than at the beginning. She could jump many more times without getting tired, too.

When you don't use your muscles enough, they can't do much for you. When you keep in shape, you can move fast and run far. You have enough energy for work and games. Your body can do many of the things you want it to do.

Exercising Safely

You must be careful to exercise safely. Not every person needs the same amount of exercise. Check with your doctor or school nurse to find out how much exercise is right for you. Then, start out slowly. Do just a little exercise each day. In two or three months, you can exercise safely for longer periods of time.

You Can Reach Goals

Liza and Noah went to camp. Every day they spent 30 minutes in the water. Liza wanted to be able to swim longer distances. Noah wanted to learn to dive. Both practiced reaching their **goals.** A goal is something you want that you work to reach. At the end of camp, Liza and Noah's parents came to see their children. Liza swam all the way across the pool. Noah dove off the low diving board. Their parents were very proud. So were Liza and <u>Noah</u>.

<u>I</u>t is fun to set goals for yourself. You can work on new skills. You can get better at doing old ones. Little by little, you can set harder goals for yourself.

Setting Exercise Goals for Yourself

Think about some of the activities that help you get your exercise. Which of these activities would you like to do better? Choose one or two and set a new goal for yourself. Practice. See how much you improve.

How did setting exercise goals help Liza and Noah?

Why might this girl be feeling good about herself? How can you tell?

You Can Feel Good About Yourself

Ralph practices jumping forward as far as he can. Each day, he jumps a little farther than he did the day before.

Bobbie is going ice skating for the first time. The ice feels slippery. Bobbie's skates wobble a lot, too. But Bobbie's muscles are strong. She has learned to do many things with her body. Bobbie knows she will learn to ice skate, too.

Every time your body does something new, you get a good feeling about yourself. Even when you learn one small thing, you can feel good about it.

REVIEW IT NOW

1. What is muscle tone?
2. Why is it important to use your muscles regularly?
3. How does setting exercise goals help you keep your body in good shape?

DIFFERENT WAYS TO EXERCISE

Some people think they can exercise only in a gym. Others think they can exercise only when they play active games outside with their friends. But people can exercise alone as well as with others. And they can exercise inside as well as outside.

When You Are Alone

There are many ways to exercise when you are by yourself. Bonnie throws a basketball into a ring behind her house. Russ sometimes practices cartwheels and headstands on his lawn.

Scott walks to a lot of places by himself. He walks back and forth to school. He walks to friends' houses. He walks to the store for his family. This week, Scott decided to walk fast wherever he goes. Walking fast is fun. It is also a good way to exercise when you are alone. Walking fast makes your heart and lungs work harder. It makes your leg muscles work harder, too.

What are some other ways this girl could exercise when she is by herself?

Thinking of Ways to Become More Active

Become more active. Exercise instead of watching TV. When you can, walk instead of being driven places. Ride your bike to do errands or for fun. Learn a new sport. Ask an adult to take you for a hike. Think of new ways that you can become more active.

Trying New Activities

For some games and activities, you need equipment. For others you don't need any. Think of three games that require little or no equipment. Write them down. Try these activities. Do you think these are good exercise? Why?

How are these boys helping their hearts and lungs?

When You Are with Others

You can be active in many ways with other people. Sometimes you might play ball games like basketball or soccer. Other times, you might do group activities like playing tag or running a relay race.

Mitchell is on a volleyball team. He and his team meet at least once a week to play another team. Running around the volleyball court helps make Mitchell's leg muscles strong. Playing volleyball gives his heart and lungs a good workout too.

Claire and her friends often play Follow the Leader. Every move must be a hop, skip, or jump. Hopping, skipping, and jumping make their hearts and lungs work hard.

Whether you play on a team or take part in group activities, you are using your body in ways that help to keep you healthy.

Aerobic Dance Teacher

If you enjoy exercise, music, and teaching, you may want to become an *aerobic dance teacher.* Aerobic dancing exercises your whole body. It also strengthens your heart and helps your breathe deeper. Aerobic dancing uses music to add rhythm to the exercises.

To become an aerobic dance teacher, you must be in very good physical condition. Courses in music and physical education are helpful. Most aerobic dance teachers train with an experienced teacher first. To learn more about being an aerobic dance teacher, write to the President's Council on Physical Fitness and Sports, 400 6th Street SW, Washington, DC 20201.

Health Career

You can get exercise outside or inside. Outside, you have more space for running. Outdoors, you are probably allowed to make more noise as well.

Alvin lives in a small house. He can go out and play in his yard. The sidewalk in front of his house is not busy, so he can play there, too.

Dotty lives in an apartment house in a city. She can't play outside in the busy streets. Dotty meets her friends in the nearby playground. There, they can be active and safe at the same time.

You can also get exercise when you play indoors. Bert shoots baskets with his sister. They throw a foam rubber ball into a plastic basket that hangs on Bert's door. Carol loves to turn on the radio, or put on a record, and dance to the music. Indoors is a very good place for dancing. Dancing can be an enjoyable way to exercise.

How are these boys getting exercise outdoors? In what ways could they exercise indoors as well?

Other exercises you can do indoors are **calisthenics.** These are sets of exercises you do regularly. Calisthenics can be done without equipment. They should be done for at least 15 minutes at a time. Before calisthenics, you should do stretching exercises. Stretching helps your body to get ready for the exercises you will do. When you finish calisthenics, you need to do cooling-down exercises, also. These help your body to cool down slowly. There are stretching and cooling-down exercises in the *Exercise Handbook* at the back of this book. It begins on page 216.

Why is calisthenics a good way to exercise?

Doing Face Calisthenics

Did you know that you have more than 100 muscles in your face alone? It takes 34 muscles to frown and 13 muscles to smile! See how many things you can do with the muscles of your face. Raise your eyebrows. Wrinkle up your nose. Try twisting your lips around.

REVIEW IT NOW

1. Why is walking fast a good exercise?
2. Why is stretching important when exercising?
3. What do you need to do when you finish exercising?

FINDING WAYS TO EXERCISE

There are many ways to exercise during your day. You can use time before school begins. You can use time after school, too. You may seem to have less time than you would like. But you can find ways to exercise that you may not have thought of.

Fitting Exercise into Your Day

Eban and Jared get to school early. Eban runs around the schoolyard as many times as he can. Jared stands near a wall and jumps high in the air. He sees where his fingers touch the wall. Each day Jared tries to beat his record from the day before.

Ted, Cindy, and Lionel each have two parents who work. Ted and Cindy have chores to do after school. Lionel's parents like him to finish his homework before he does anything else.

One of Ted's after-school jobs is dusting the furniture. He exercises his whole body while he works. Ted stretches and reaches and bends.

How is Jared finding a way to exercise during a busy day?

Keeping an Exercise Record

Keep an exercise record. Do some of the exercises in the *Exercise Handbook*. List them. Write the date you begin. Write the number of times you do each exercise. Write how the exercises make you feel (use words such as "great," "good," "okay," "tired"). Do the exercises regularly. After one month, check your record. What changes have taken place? Are you exercising longer? Do you find the exercises easier to do? Do you have more energy?

Cindy walks her dog, Prince, every afternoon. She and Prince walk very fast for part of the time. They run for part of the time, too. Both Cindy and Prince are getting exercise that helps them to be healthy.

If you don't have much free time, you have to think carefully about getting enough exercise. You should try to exercise for at least 15 minutes at a time to make your heart and lungs stronger.

You may want to plan a regular program of exercises. Look at the *Exercise Handbook* in the back of this book. It begins on page 216. It gives some exercises you can do. Be sure to do stretching and cooling-down exercises as part of your program.

Be sure your exercise program includes enough time to rest. Exercising uses up energy. Resting helps your body to gain new energy. Sometimes your muscles can tighten up. Resting helps your muscles relax. Then your muscles loosen up. This helps your whole body to relax. You can rest by lying down and closing your eyes. You can also rest by just sitting quietly.

Exercising As You Do Your Chores

What chores do you do in your house? How can you give your body more of a workout while you do what you have to do? List your jobs. Next to each one, write action words such as "bend," "stretch," and "reach". Try these actions as you do your chores.

How does walking her dog every afternoon help keep Cindy healthy?

Toshiko d'Elia

Focus On

When Toshiko d'Elia was 40 years old, she tried climbing Mt. Rainier in the state of Washington. Toshiko collapsed during the climb. Then she decided to get into better shape.

Now Toshiko runs two or three *marathon races* every year. A marathon race is a little more than 26 miles (42 kilometers). Toshiko has set records as one of the fastest runners over 50 years old. She teaches running at schools in the United States and Japan. Toshiko advises people to have a lifetime exercise plan. She enjoys organizing races for children.

Knowing When to Exercise Less

There are times when you should cut down on your usual activities. When you are ill, it is a good idea to rest. Exercise uses up energy. Your body needs its energy to help make you well. You should also be sure you are well before you become as active as you usually are.

Steffie broke her wrist. She wore a cast for many weeks. She had to keep her arm still, so it could heal. Now the cast is off. Steffie's arm muscles lost some of their tone. Steffie is getting **physical therapy.** Physical therapy can be special light exercises to help make a part of the body strong again.

Sometimes a person is not able to take part in regular activities or games. A doctor can give advice about what activities are right for a person. There are also specially trained people called **physical therapists.** They can help find activities for people with special physical problems.

This boy is getting physical therapy to help make certain muscles stronger.

What way of exercising has this family found to enjoy? What other kinds of exercise might they find to enjoy?

Finding Out What You Enjoy

There are many ways to exercise. You can find out what you enjoy by trying different activities. You might enjoy bicycle riding with a friend more than using equipment in a gym. You may love dancing. But you may not enjoy many team sports. Everyone can find ways to exercise that are fun.

REVIEW IT NOW

1. What are some ways to exercise during a busy day?
2. What is physical therapy?

Planning a Family Exercise Outing

There are many exercise activities that a whole family can do together. Think about the activities your family likes to do. Discuss these questions together to help plan a family exercise outing.

Beyond the Classroom

- What kinds of exercise do you most enjoy?
- Do you have sports equipment like bicycles and balls? Is there a swimming pool available? Would you prefer activities like short hikes that don't require much equipment?
- Which activities can everyone in the family do?

Have a wonderful time!

To Help You Review

Checking Your Understanding

Write the numbers from 1 to 12 on your paper. After each number, write the answer to the question. Page numbers in ( ) tell you where to look in the chapter if you need help.

1. How do your muscles help your bones to move? (**101**)
2. What part of your body sends messages to your muscles? (**102**)
3. What do your muscles use when they work hard? (**102**)
4. What happens to your heart when you run? (**103**)
5. What happens to your breathing when you run? (**103**)
6. Why does exercising help you to feel more wide awake? (**104**)
7. What happens to your heart when you exercise regularly? (**106**)
8. What happens to your lungs when you exercise regularly? (**106**)
9. How do you help your muscles when you exercise regularly? (**106**)
10. What are some ways you can get exercise when you are alone? (**109**)
11. What are some ways you can get exercise when you are with others? (**110**)
12. When should you cut down on your regular activities? (**117**)

Checking Your Health Vocabulary

Write the numbers from 1 to 3 on your paper. After each number, write the letter of the meaning for the word or words. Page numbers in ( ) tell you where to look in the chapter if you need help.

1. tissues (**101**)
2. muscles (**101**)
3. muscle tone (**106**)

a. firmness of muscles
b. groups of tissues that help your body move
c. groups of the same kinds of cells that work together

Write the numbers from 4 to 8 on your paper. Read each sentence and fill in the missing word or words. Page numbers in ( ) tell you where to look in the chapter if you need help.

4. An important way to be healthy is to get regular _____ . (**100**)
5. Your _____ helps give your body its shape. (**101**)
6. Setting _____ for yourself can help you get better at skills. (**107**)
7. Sets of exercises you do regularly are _____ . (**113**)
8. Special help that someone with a physical problem can get is _____ _____ . (**117**)

Practice Test

True or False?

Write the numbers from 1 to 15 on your paper. After each number, write *T* if the sentence is *true*. Write *F* if it is *false*. Rewrite each false sentence to make it true.

1. Regular exercise can be done only in a gym.
2. Your skeleton helps give your body its shape.
3. Your body needs more oxygen when you exercise.
4. Your muscles move with the help of your bones.
5. The more your muscles work, the less energy they need.
6. After regular exercise, your heart gets stronger, but your lungs get weaker.
7. Exercise is always tiring.
8. It can feel good to learn how to use your body in a new way.
9. Exercising by yourself is a waste of time.
10. Stretching and cooling down are parts of exercising.
11. Calisthenics is the only form of exercise you can do indoors.
12. Calisthenics should be done for at least 15 minutes at a time.
13. There is never a good reason to cut back on your activities.
14. Muscles can lose some of their firmness if they are not used regularly.
15. There are exercises that everyone can enjoy.

Complete the Sentence

Write the numbers from 16 to 20 on your paper. After each number, copy the sentence and fill in the missing word or words.

16. One way to have a healthy body is to get _____ exercise.
17. Exercise can make your _____ pump harder.
18. An exercise program should include time to _____ and _____ .
19. Calisthenics are exercises you can easily do _____ .
20. A _____ _____ helps find activities for people with special problems.

Learning More

For You to Do

1. Set an exercise goal for yourself. You may choose to try a new activity. Maybe you have been wanting to learn to skate. Or you may want to improve an activity you already do. Perhaps you can pedal your bicycle farther. Maybe you can learn a new swimming stroke. Once you have reached your goal, set a new one.

2. Teach a younger child a simple exercise or sport. Perhaps you can show him or her how to catch a ball or do a sit-up. Doing exercises like jumping jacks might also be a good choice. Be prepared to be patient and encouraging.

For You to Find Out

1. Look through the biography section of your library. Find the name of an interesting sports person or dancer. Find out how that person became interested in the activity. Did the person have any training as a child for this career?

2. Look through a dictionary or an encyclopedia. Find out about the sports that use the piece of equipment below:
   - wicket
   - oar
   - bat
   - net
   - puck
   - racquet

For You to Read

Here are some books you can look for in your school or public library. They will help you to find out more about exercising for health and fun.

Krementz, Jill. *A Very Young Gymnast.* Knopf, 1978.

Neimark, Paul. *Hiking and Exploring.* Children's Press, 1981.

Nelson, Esther L. *Movement Games—For Children of All Ages.* Sterling, 1977.

CHAPTER 6

Learning About Illness

Everyone becomes ill from time to time. When you are ill, your body doesn't work as it should. You may not want to eat or play or do much of anything.

A doctor may give you medicine to fight your illness. Or your body may fight the illness by itself. Your body works hard to keep you healthy. It works hard to make you healthy again if you become ill.

There are many things you can do so that you don't become ill very often. If you do become ill, you can do things to help yourself get well.

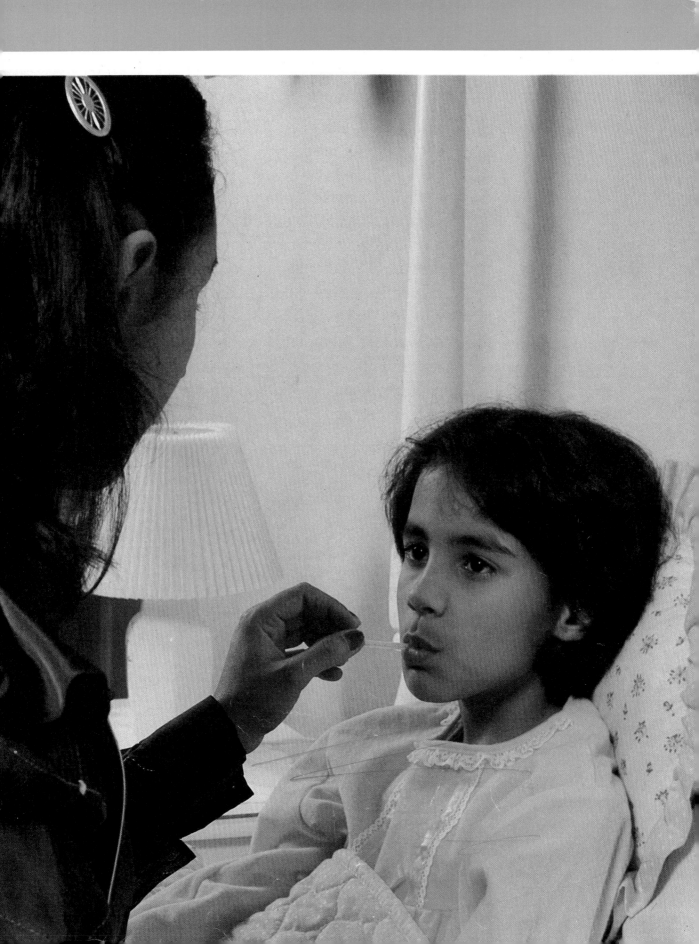

Fever

The extra heat of a fever helps your body when you are ill. The heat makes your blood move more quickly around your body. Your blood brings more nutrients and other things your body needs to fight the illness.

Why did Mrs. Valdez think Patty might be ill?

KNOWING WHEN YOU MAY BE ILL

Patty loves chicken. At dinner she just picked at her piece. "Don't you feel well?" her father asked. Patty said her head hurt. She said she also felt aches all over. Her throat was feeling scratchy, too.

Patty's mother put her to bed early. In the morning, Patty still did not feel well. Mrs. Valdez took her daughter's temperature. It was higher than normal. A body temperature that is higher than normal is a **fever.** Mrs. Valdez called a doctor.

Mrs. Valdez knew Patty was ill because of her **symptoms.** Symptoms are signs that something is wrong in the body. Your body has many ways to let you know that something is wrong.

Causes of Some Illnesses

Some illnesses are caused by harmful germs. One group of germs that can cause illnesses is **bacteria.** Bacteria need food and water to live. Another kind of germ is a **virus.** Viruses are even smaller than bacteria. Viruses kill living cells in order to live.

How Your Body Fights Back

Your body protects itself against harmful germs with its **white blood cells.** These are certain cells in your blood. They fight harmful germs when they get into your body.

What happens when there are too many germs for your white blood cells to handle? Then your body makes **antibodies.** Antibodies surround germs. They stop them from getting what they need from your cells. Then the white blood cells can kill the germs.

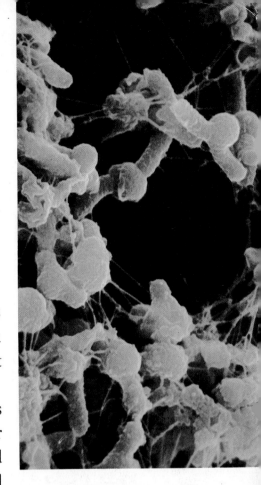

How do antibodies help your body fight harmful germs like these?

REVIEW IT NOW

---

1. What are symptoms?
2. What are two ways your body fights illness?

127

SOME ILLNESSES YOU CAN CATCH

Some illnesses are passed from one person to another. These are called **communicable illnesses.**

Chicken Pox

Millie woke up with a headache and achiness. She also had a fever. Her parents kept her home from school. The next day, Millie began to get small, red spots on her face and body. First, she got itchy blisters. Then, the blisters broke. Each blister formed a red crust, or scab. Millie had chicken pox. Chicken pox is an illness caused by a virus.

The itchy scabs bothered Millie. Her father put something on them to stop the itching. He didn't want Millie to scratch the scabs. Scabs help keep germs out of a spot that is healing.

Some other children in Millie's school also had chicken pox. They stayed home, too, until they were well. This helped to keep even more children from catching the illness.

Why might this girl have to stay home until she is well?

Electronic Read-Out Thermometers

You have probably had your temperature taken to check for fever. Most likely, you held a glass thermometer under your tongue. You probably had to wait several minutes until the correct temperature was shown. Then an adult read the temperature shown in the glass tube.

Now there is a much easier way to take temperatures. It can be done with *electronic read-out thermometers.* With some of these thermometers, you hold a thin piece of plastic under your tongue. In just seven seconds you can easily read your correct temperature in bright numerals. A new, clean piece of plastic is used for each patient. Today, most electronic thermometers are used in hospitals and clinics.

Health Today

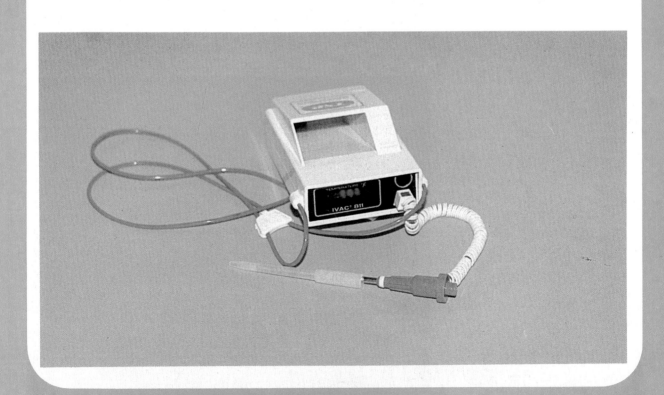

Colds are caused by different viruses. Colds can affect your nose, throat, and lungs. When you have a cold, you may have a stuffy or runny nose. Your throat may feel scratchy. You may also have a cough. Sometimes you may have a fever and chills.

Colds can last for a few days or much longer. Colds are communicable. They can easily be spread by sneezes and coughs. If you have a cold, be careful not to spread the cold viruses to others.

Influenza is known as "flu." Flu is caused by many different kinds of viruses. Flu can be mild or serious. It may begin with symptoms of a cold. You may have chills, fever, and a headache. You may not be very hungry. The flu can make you feel very tired. There is nothing you can take to kill a flu virus. But you can do some things to feel better. Get plenty of rest. Drink lots of liquids. Flu might last several days.

How is this girl helping to keep her cold from spreading to others?

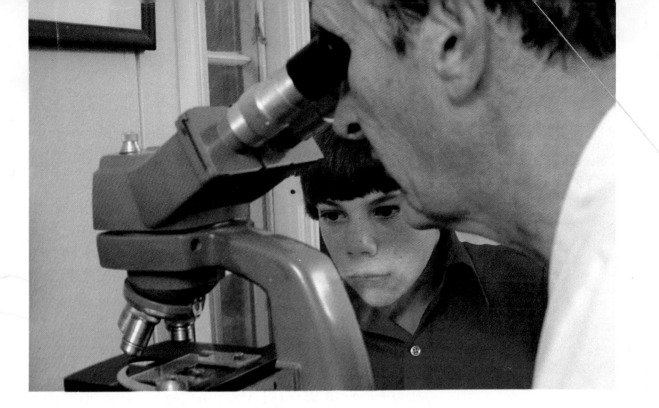

Strep Throat

Why might this doctor be checking germs under a microscope?

One kind of sore throat is called a strep throat. It is caused by certain bacteria that grow in your throat. A strep throat can feel very sore. Your throat can become very red and swollen. A strep throat is also very communicable. It can pass quickly from one person to another.

A strep throat can make you very ill. It should be treated right away. Tell an adult if your throat hurts. A doctor or nurse can collect germs from your throat. The germs can be checked under a microscope. The doctor or nurse can tell if you have strep bacteria.

REVIEW IT NOW

1. What is a communicable illness?
2. What are some communicable illnesses?

Focus On

Erma McKenzie

Erma McKenzie has worked in a hospital laboratory for 15 years. She does many tests for people. Now she has a new way to record all the tests she does. Erma uses a computer.

One test Erma does is a *throat culture.* She gently wipes a cotton swab near the back of a person's throat. Then, the swab is rubbed onto a special, jellylike material in the laboratory. Germs may grow on the material in about two days. If harmful germs grow, the person's doctor may give medicine to stop an illness. Every time Erma does a test, she puts the person's name and the name of the test into the computer. Later she will put in the results.

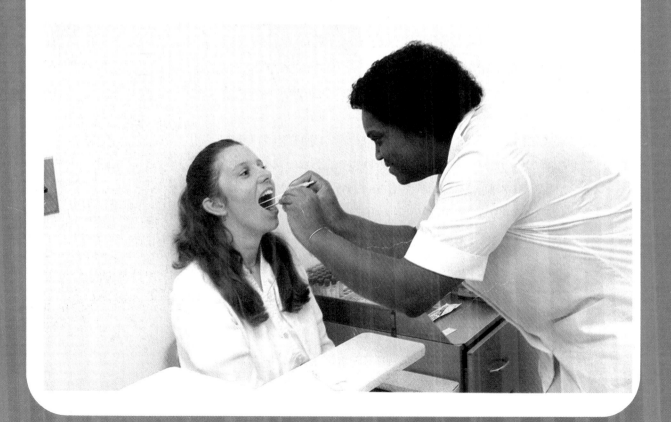

SOME ILLNESSES YOU CANNOT CATCH

Many illnesses are not caused by germs. You cannot catch these illnesses.

Allergies

Sunday, Glen Feller woke up with red, itchy bumps on his face and chest. Glen's father took him to the emergency room of the nearby hospital.

A nurse examined Glen's body right away. Then the doctor checked Glen. The doctor told Glen that the itchy bumps might have been caused by some kind of food. Glen and his father thought about what they had eaten the day before. Glen did remember eating something he had never eaten before.

The doctor gave Glen something to make the itchy bumps go away. She then told Glen to avoid eating the food that may have caused the bumps.

Glen has a food **allergy.** An allergy is the body's unusual reaction to something. Some people are allergic to certain fruits. They can also be allergic to milk, eggs, wheat, and some kinds of fish. Almost any food can be the cause of an allergy.

The bumps that broke out on Glen's body are just one symptom of an allergy. When Polly gets near a cat or dog, her nose itches. She also sneezes. Polly may be allergic to dog and cat fur.

Some people are allergic to dust. Others are allergic to certain pills given for some illnesses. Still others are allergic to plant pollen. Pollen is the part of a plant that makes the seeds. Pollen travels through the air. When some people breathe in pollen, their bodies react to it.

Is Beth allergic to cat fur? How can you tell?

When you have an allergy, your body makes antibodies. These antibodies make your body react to the things to which you are allergic.

Diabetes

Another illness you cannot catch is **diabetes.**

After you eat, nutrients from food are carried by your blood to your cells. Some nutrients are burned right away in your cells to give you energy. Some are stored. One nutrient your cells need to burn for energy is a form of sugar.

When people have diabetes, this sugar does not go into their cells. Instead, it stays in the blood. Too much sugar in the blood can make people ill.

Doctors can treat diabetes with certain pills. They can also give "shots," or injections. The injections are a liquid. The liquid helps the cells take in the sugar from the blood. Many people take these injections every day. Often, people are taught to give themselves the shots. Sometimes, doctors also tell people with diabetes to eat a special diet to help control their illness.

REVIEW IT NOW

1. What is an allergy?
2. What are some things that can be the cause of an allergy?
3. How can doctors treat diabetes?

Allergist

A doctor who treats allergies is an *allergist.* An allergist finds out the things that cause a person's allergy. To do this, an allergist injects bits of things like dust and feathers under the skin. An allergist may give special shots to help lessen a person's unusual reaction. For food allergies, an allergist carefully controls a person's diet.

Allergists need four years of college. Then they need four years of medical school, followed by one or more years of special training. To learn more about being an allergist, write to the American Academy of Allergy and Immunology, 611 East Wells Street, Milwaukee, WI 53202.

Health Career

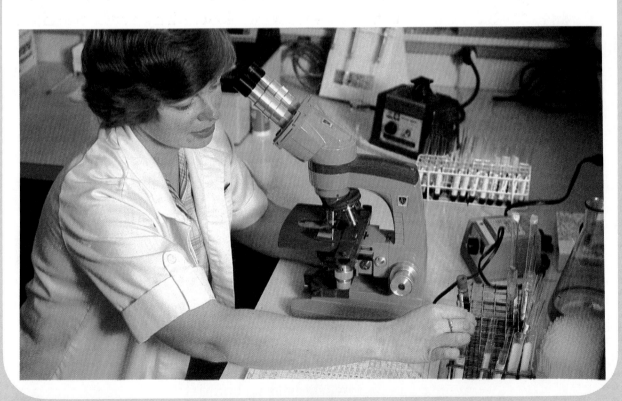

PREVENTING ILLNESSES

Many years ago, certain communicable illnesses were common. Today, the doctor can give you **medicines** to make sure you don't get these illnesses. Medicines can help prevent illnesses. They can also help make you well when you are ill.

Getting Immunizations

Communicable Illnesses for Which There Are Vaccines
Diphtheria
Mumps
Pertussis (whooping cough)
Polio
Rubeola (2-week measles)
Rubella (3-day measles)
Tetanus

There are medicines that can help make you **immune** to certain illnesses. When you are immune to an illness, the germ that causes it has no power to make you ill.

To help make you immune, the doctor or nurse gives **immunizations.** Some immunizations are given to you by a shot. Some you swallow in liquid form. The medicine in immunizations is a **vaccine.** A vaccine puts some germs of a certain kind into your body. There aren't enough germs to make you ill. Instead, your body makes antibodies against them. The antibodies will help make you immune to that kind of germ.

Certain illnesses are communicable. Some can be very serious. These are two reasons why immunizations are very important. Also, in most states, children can't begin school unless they get all the immunizations they should have. The doctor or school nurse often tells parents when more immunizations are due. These are called **boosters.**

Getting Checkups

The doctor can find out if everything in your body is working as it should. First, he or she may ask you and your parents questions about your health. The doctor may also ask about the health of your family. The doctor keeps a record of what he or she learns. You may also have your throat, eyes, nose, ears, heart, and lungs checked. The doctor also keeps a record of your growth.

Getting Food, Rest, and Exercise

Food, rest, and exercise are important in keeping you healthy. Eating healthful foods each day will help make your cells stronger. Getting plenty of exercise helps, too. If you get enough rest and sleep, your cells will have the energy they need to fight harmful germs.

Dressing Properly

It is also important to protect your body by dressing properly. If your body gets too cold, your cells can become too weak to protect you from harmful germs. You can help your body by dressing warmly in cold weather.

How does dressing for rainy weather help protect these children from illnesses?

When it is rainy or snowy, wear clothing that will keep you dry as well as warm. If you get chilled, your body can get too cold. In hot weather, wear cool, light clothing. When you are too hot, your body gets overheated. It needs to cool down.

Keeping away from Germs

Keeping yourself clean is a good way to get rid of many germs. It is especially important to wash your hands before eating and after using the toilet. Another way to avoid germs is to stay away from people with bad colds or other communicable illnesses.

Reporting Symptoms

Let an adult know if you don't feel well. It is important to treat an illness right away. You can help keep an illness from lasting a long time by treating it right away. You can also help keep it from getting worse. You can help protect other people from getting the illness, too.

For what kind of weather is this girl dressed in each picture?

REVIEW IT NOW

1. How do immunizations help you?
2. Why should you dress warmly in cold weather?
3. What are some things you can do to try to avoid an illness?

WHAT TO DO WHEN YOU ARE ILL

Luther was in school when he began to feel ill. He told the school nurse. She called his mother. Luther's mother came to take him home early.

Rest and Drink Plenty of Liquids

Luther spent the next few days in bed. At first, he felt tired. So he got plenty of rest. While he rested, his body used its energy to fight his illness.

On the first day, Luther had a fever. His mother gave him medicine to lower his fever and make him feel better. She fed him food that was easy to digest. That way, Luther's body would not use up a lot of energy digesting his food. She also gave him plenty of juices and other liquids to drink. Luther's mother knew that liquids would help put back water that Luther lost when he had a fever.

How will getting plenty of rest and drinking plenty of liquids help Luther to get well?

Why is it important not to have extra visitors when you are ill?

Try Not to Spread Germs

Luther's illness could easily be passed on to someone else. So Luther didn't have extra visitors. He was careful to cover his mouth and nose when he sneezed or coughed. He put his used tissues in a bag, so his germs wouldn't spread. He washed his hands more often. He didn't want to send germs back into his body.

Now, Luther is feeling much better. If he feels good during the weekend, he will go back to school.

REVIEW IT NOW

1. What are four things that may help you when you are ill?
2. What four things can you do to keep from passing germs on to others?

Keeping a Medical History

It is a good idea to keep a record of the illnesses you have had. There are some illnesses you can get only once. Many can usually be prevented with immunizations. Keeping a record of your illnesses and immunizations will help you to know which illnesses you probably will not get. Such information may help your doctor treat you if you become ill.

Make a chart like the one below. Ask an adult in your family to help with the information. Be sure to keep the facts up to date. Keep your medical history in a safe place.

Beyond the Classroom

Medical History		
Name _Jorge_ Age _8_ Date _January 8, 1983_		
Illness	Year of Illness	Year of Immunization
chicken pox	1982	
flu		
mumps		1977
strep throat	1981	
rubella (3-day measles)		1977
rubeola (2-week measles)		1977
diphtheria, tetanus, and pertussis		3 times in 1975 Booster shots in 1976 and 1980
polio		3 times in 1976 Booster shots in 1976 and 1980

To Help You Review

Checking Your Understanding

Write the numbers from 1 to 11 on your paper. After each number, write the answer to the question. Page numbers in ( ) tell you where to look in the chapter if you need help.

1. What do symptoms tell you? (**126**)
2. What causes some illnesses? (**127**)
3. What are two ways your body fights an illness? (**127**)
4. What are some symptoms of chicken pox? (**128**)
5. How do the scabs from chicken pox help your body? (**128**)
6. How can colds be spread to others? (**130**)
7. If you have the flu, what two things can you do to feel better? (**130**)
8. What are some symptoms of allergies? (**133**)
9. How can diabetes be treated? (**134**)
10. Why is it important to have immunizations? (**136**)
11. What are some ways to help keep yourself from becoming ill? (**136-138**)

Checking Your Health Vocabulary

Write the numbers from 1 to 6 on your paper. After each number, write the letter of the meaning for the word or words. Page numbers in ( ) tell you where to look in the chapter if you need help.

1. fever (**126**)
2. symptoms (**126**)
3. virus (**127**)
4. communicable illnesses (**128**)
5. medicines (**136**)
6. immunizations (**136**)

a. things that can help prevent illness or help make you well when you are ill
b. signs that something is wrong in the body
c. a germ that kills cells in order to live
d. vaccines given by injection or swallowed
e. a body temperature that is higher than normal
f. illnesses that can be passed from one person to another

Write the numbers from 7 to 12 on your paper. Then write a sentence that explains the meaning of each word or words. Page numbers in ( ) tell you where to look in the chapter if you need help.

7. white blood cells (**127**)
8. bacteria (**127**)
9. allergy (**133**)
10. vaccine (**136**)
11. immune (**136**)
12. boosters (**136**)

Practice Test

True or False?

Write the numbers from 1 to 15 on your paper. After each number, write *T* if the sentence is *true*. Write *F* if it is *false*. Rewrite each false sentence to make it true.

1. Symptoms are warning signs of illness.
2. Your body is helpless against germs.
3. When you have chicken pox, you get blisters that form scabs.
4. A cold is not a communicable illness.
5. Cold symptoms are always followed by the flu.
6. There is nothing you can take to kill a flu virus.
7. Doctors can check for strep throat germs.
8. Allergies are communicable.
9. Many allergies are caused by the pollen of plants.
10. Almost any food can be the cause of an allergy.
11. Diabetes is an illness of the skin.
12. You can become immune to all illnesses.
13. Vaccines are medicines that put some germs into your body.
14. All illnesses can be prevented.
15. When you have a fever, it is important to drink liquids.

Complete the Sentence

Write the numbers from 16 to 20 on your paper. After each number, copy the sentence and fill in the missing word.

16. When your body _____ goes way up, you have a fever.
17. Your body makes _____ that help fight germs.
18. Diabetes can be treated with pills or shots and sometimes with a special _____ .
19. An allergy can be uncomfortable, but it is not _____ .
20. You can help prevent illness by dressing _____ in cold weather.

Learning More

For You to Do

1. Immunizations have worked to save thousands of lives. Look up smallpox in an encyclopedia. You may also find it in the card catalogue in the library. Find out how this illness has been stopped. Write a report about it. Explain what smallpox is. Then tell how it affected people. Tell how people today are protected from this illness.

2. Make a poster that reminds people to get immunizations. Use some bright colors and catchy words. Also remember to explain what immunizations are. You may want to ask to exhibit the poster in your school library.

For You to Find Out

1. Each person below helped fight illness in an important way. Use library books or an encyclopedia. Find out how each person helped. (Remember to look up each person using the last name.)
   - Edward Jenner
   - Louis Pasteur
   - Rosalyn S. Yalow

2. Anton van Leeuwenhoek lived from 1632 to 1723. He made many of the first microscopes. He carefully described germs for the first time. Use library books or an encyclopedia. Find out what van Leeuwenhoek's microscope looked like. Compare it with pictures of a modern microscope.

For You to Read

Here are some books you can look for in your school or public library. They can help you find out more about illnesses.

Cobb, Vicki. *How the Doctor Knows You're Fine.* Lippincott, 1973.

Nourse, Alan. *Lumps, Bumps, and Rashes.* Franklin Watts, 1976.

Silverstein, Alvin, and Silverstein, Virginia. *Itch, Sniffle, and Sneeze.* Four Winds, 1978.

CHAPTER 7

Drugs and Your Health

A drug is something that can change the way your body works. Some drugs can help make you well when you are sick. Others can make you more comfortable until you get well.

There are drugs in some things people drink. Drugs are also found in tobacco. These drugs can be harmful to you.

It is important to know about drugs and what they can do to your body and to your health.

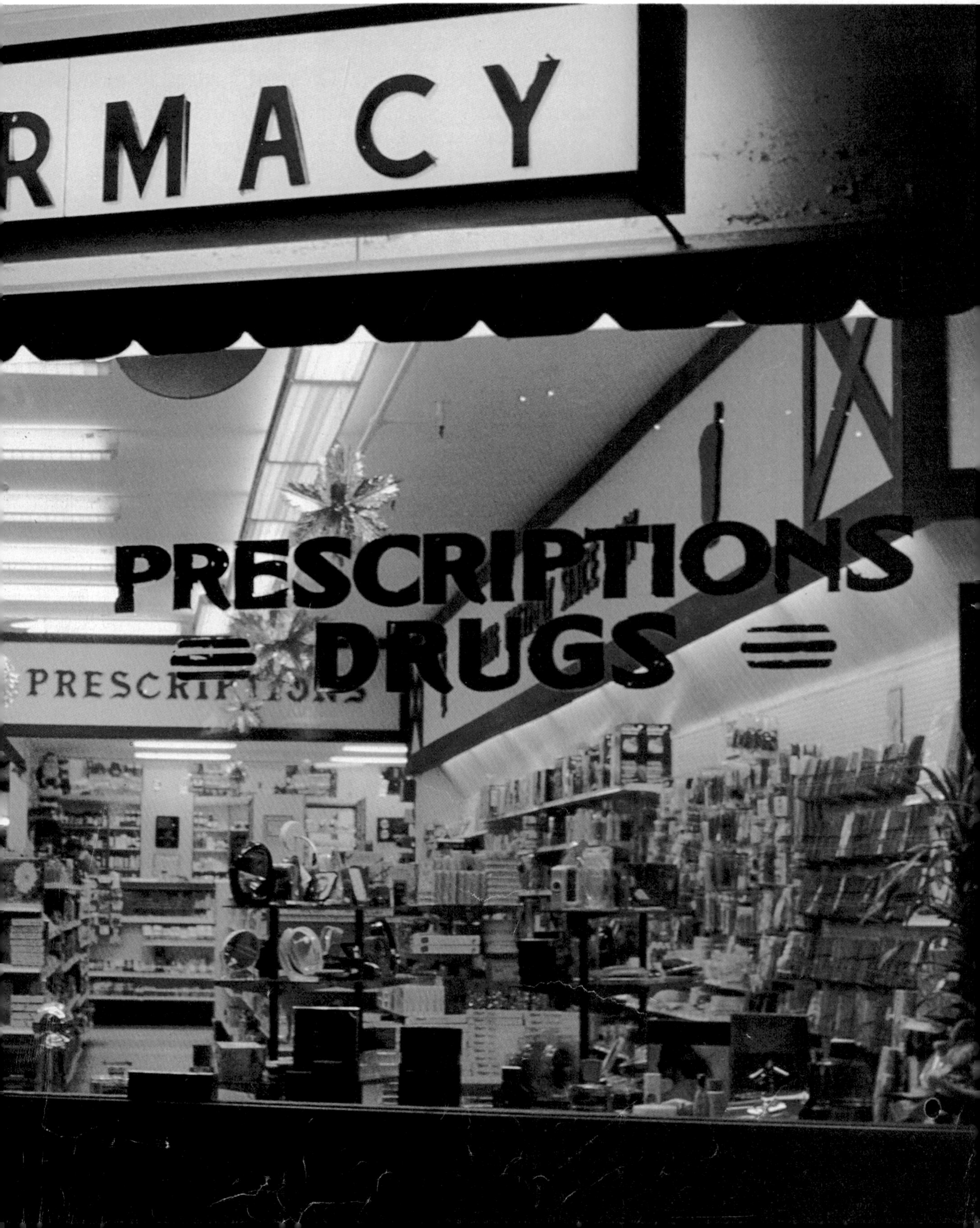
RMACY
PRESCRIPTIONS
DRUGS

You won't be surprised to learn that drugs are found in drugstores. They are also found in supermarkets and restaurants. Certain kinds of drugs may even be found in people's homes.

Drugs Can Be Found in Many Things

Brad's mother gave him some red liquid. It tasted like cherries. But it wasn't food. It was cough syrup. Cough syrup has some **drugs** in it. A drug is something other than food that can make a change in your body.

Some drugs can help you fight illnesses. These drugs are medicines. Medicines can also fight the symptoms of illnesses. The cough syrup Brad took is a medicine. It has a drug in it. The cough syrup helped stop Brad's cough.

Medicines come in many forms. Some are liquids that are injected into your body. Others you can put on your skin, such as a skin cream. Some medicines are pills or a liquid you swallow.

After You Swallow a Medicine

It takes a short time for medicine you swallow to get to your stomach and into your small intestine. It goes through your intestine walls into your bloodstream. Your blood carries the medicine to all parts of your body.

In what way will cough syrup help fight Brad's symptom?

Some people have drinks with drugs in them. Cocoa, cola, coffee, tea, wine, beer, and liquor contain drugs. These drugs don't fight illnesses. Sometimes they can have strong effects on the body.

Drugs can be helpful or harmful. How a drug is used has a lot to do with whether it will help or harm a person.

Why Certain Drugs Are Sometimes Needed

Tommy had a bad sore throat. His doctor said it was a strep throat. He told Tommy that his white blood cells needed help to fight the bacteria that were causing the strep throat. The doctor gave Tommy a drug called **penicillin.**

Penicillin is a very strong **antibiotic** drug. Antibiotics are drugs made from certain living things. They can be made from bacteria or from certain kinds of plants. Penicillin is made from a kind of plant called mold. Antibiotics attack bacteria and help stop certain illnesses from getting worse.

Look at the penicillin mold on the lemon. How does penicillin help keep certain illnesses from getting worse?

A "Wonder Drug"

When penicillin was first discovered, it was called a "wonder drug." It saved the lives of many people who would have died without it. Penicillin was discovered by a scientist named Alexander Fleming, who was studying bacteria. He grew some bacteria in a special dish. One day he noticed mold around the bacteria. The mold spread and killed the bacteria around it. The scientist called the mold penicillin. *Penicillin* means "small brush." It was called that because the cells of the mold look like little brushes.

How will the medicine Eva's mother is giving her help Eva?

Some drugs can make you feel better when you are ill. Eva had a cold. Her body ached and her nose was runny. Eva's doctor told her mother to give her some aspirin. The doctor also said Eva could have some nose drops. The drugs in these medicines did not cure Eva's cold. They stopped the symptoms of the cold. Eva felt better, but she had to stay home from school and rest for a while.

REVIEW IT NOW

1. What is a drug?
2. How are some drugs helpful to people?
3. What is an antibiotic drug?

BEING SAFE AROUND MEDICINES

Medicines can do great harm if they aren't used correctly. Medicines must be used with great care if they are to help a person to be healthy.

A person can buy many medicines without an order from a doctor. Such medicines are called **over-the-counter,** or **OTC, medicines.**

Robert had played a hard game of volleyball. His back muscles felt sore. His mother went to the drugstore. She chose an OTC medicine from the shelf. She read the directions very carefully. At home, she rubbed the medicine on Robert's back. It helped relax his muscles and made him feel better.

Sometimes a doctor writes an order for a special medicine. The doctor's order is called a **prescription.** The prescription can be filled only by a **pharmacist.** A pharmacist prepares medicine by following the doctor's prescription.

Finding Out About Medicines in the Supermarket

Have an adult help you check the medicines sold in your local supermarket. What types of medicines are there? Write down the names of three different kinds of medicines. Find out what they are used for. Share your findings with your classmates.

What should a person do before buying any over-the-counter medicine?

STOMACH COAT™

ANTACID

This bottle has a CHILD GUARD cap.
TO OPEN: Line up arrows on cap and bottle. Push cap up with thumb.
TO CLOSE: Snap cap on. Do not line up arrows.

ADULT DOSE: 1 or 2 tablets with water every 4 hours. Children's dosage in booklet.
Caution — For children under 2 years of age, see physician.
WARNING: Keep this and all medicines out of children's reach.

Some medicines can be sold only with a prescription. These are called **prescription medicines.** The pharmacist puts directions for using the medicine on its container. These directions must be read carefully.

Take Medicines Correctly

Each medicine must be used in the correct way. Medicines that aren't meant for swallowing can be poisonous. Medicines meant for swallowing must be taken in the correct amount. Too much of a medicine can be harmful. Medicines should be taken only with the direction of a parent or a doctor.

A prescription medicine often needs to be taken an exact number of times. The doctor decides the number of times a medicine should be taken. If you take a medicine for too long, it can hurt your body. If you don't take it long enough, it may not help.

It is especially harmful to take medicines you do not know anything about. Some drugs in medicines can make people very ill. Certain drugs in medicines could even cause death.

What is the correct way to use this prescription medicine? Why is it important to use medicines correctly?

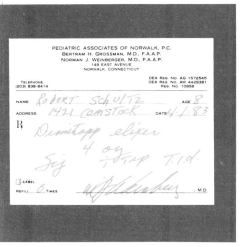

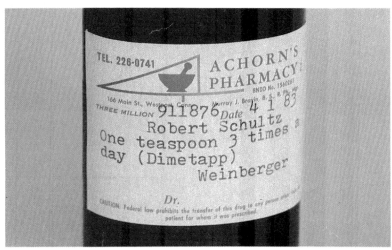

Ed Cornell

Ed Cornell is a pharmacist in Arizona. He works in a drugstore preparing and giving out medicine. Many new drugs come out each year. Ed keeps studying about medicine to learn all he can. He advises people how to stay healthy, so that they won't need medicine. He explains that children should not handle any medicines. Ed Cornell also goes to classrooms to talk to children.

Soon Ed will have a computer to keep track of the medicines sold. It will help order drugs, too. Ed's computer will even print a label with directions for using the medicine. Ed says the computer is a safety check that will help him keep people healthy.

Focus On

Why did the doctor tell Judy and her father not to use old medicines?

Be Careful with Old Medicines

Dr. Phelps wrote out a prescription for Judy Roth. Mr. Roth told the doctor he had the same medicine at home. He wondered whether the old medicine would be just as good for Judy. Dr. Phelps said it wouldn't, and she explained why. When medicines get old, they change. Some lose their strength. Then they have no power to help anyone. Some medicines get stronger as they get older. They can be harmful to take.

Old prescription medicines may have been meant for someone else. Medicines meant for one person should never be taken by someone else. Everyone is different. People are different sizes and ages. The doctor orders medicine for people based on their size and age. People are different inside, too. Some medicines may be right for one person. They may be much too strong for someone else.

Poison Control Centers

Twenty-four hours a day, seven days a week, people call more than 325 Poison Control Centers in the United States. Immediately, experts tell exactly what to do if someone has swallowed something that is poisonous. Most of the poisons are drugs, plants, and household cleaners.

The Poison Control Centers say people should call them first. Many life-saving things are right in the home. When calling a Poison Control Center, tell: (1) what was swallowed; (2) how long ago it happened; (3) how the person is feeling; (4) whether the person is a child or an adult. Poison Control Centers answer over 1½ million calls a year.

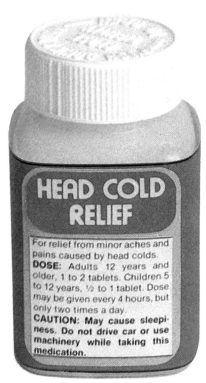

What side effect is listed on this medicine label?

Read Labels and Packages

Every medicine comes with directions and other information. Most of this information is on the label. Part of it is on the package. It is important that people read this information carefully.

Over-the-counter labels tell what drugs are in medicines. They tell how to use the medicine and how much to take. OTC labels also tell how often to take the medicine and for how long to take it.

Some drugs in medicines may cause unneeded changes in the body. These changes are known as **side effects.** A cold pill may clear up a stuffy nose. It also may make you sleepy. Labels and packages warn about the possible side effects of a drug.

Keep Small Children away from Medicines

Joel's baby sister had a rash. His mother put some special cream on the rash. The baby reached for the tube of cream. Joel's mother moved the tube out of the baby's reach. She knew the baby might become ill if she swallowed the cream.

Small children sometimes mistake pills for candy. This kind of mistake can be dangerous. Many medicines come in bottles with child-proof caps. Children cannot take them off easily.

REVIEW IT NOW

1. What are some important ways to be careful when you are thinking of using medicines?
2. Why should medicine be taken only with the direction of a parent or doctor?

DRUGS THAT ARE NOT SAFE TO USE

The Lewis family is finishing breakfast. Mrs. Lewis is drinking coffee. Mr. Lewis is drinking tea. Natalie usually has milk with breakfast. Today she is drinking a cup of cocoa. Coffee, tea, and cocoa all have a drug in them. Each contains a drug called **caffeine.** Most cola drinks contain caffeine, too.

Another drug in things people drink is **alcohol.** This drug is found in beer, wine, and liquor. Tobacco also contains drugs. Two drugs in tobacco smoke are **tar** and **nicotine.**

Caffeine

Mr. Lewis likes a few cups of coffee or tea during the day. But he sometimes finds that coffee and tea make him feel strange. Then he knows he has had too much of these drinks. Sometimes he drinks tea or coffee that does not contain caffeine. Often, he may drink fruit juice, instead.

How are these people cutting down on caffeine?

Why does too much coffee or tea make Mr. Lewis feel strange? Caffeine in coffee or tea can make the heart beat too fast. It can make a person feel jumpy. Sometimes it can even make a person too jumpy to sleep well at night.

There are coffees and teas that are made without caffeine. There are cola drinks without caffeine, too. Cutting down on caffeine is one way a person can feel better and be healthier.

Alcohol

Alcohol can cause very serious changes in a drinker's body.

Alcohol goes quickly into a person's blood. Through the blood, it reaches the brain in just minutes. What alcohol does to the brain causes many of the changes that can happen to the drinker.

Drinking alcohol can make a person feel tired and dizzy. It can make everything seem blurred. A person who drinks too much alcohol may not be able to walk straight. He or she may not be able to stand up at all. Alcohol can make it very hard to think clearly, too. Sometimes, a person who has had too much alcohol cannot remember things that have happened. Many people do not know when they have had too much alcohol. Even a little alcohol may be harmful.

Someone who has been drinking alcohol should not drive a car. Many road deaths are caused by drivers who have been drinking alcohol. These drivers couldn't see or think clearly. They weren't able to steer their cars correctly, either.

How might the driver of this car feel about people driving after drinking alcohol? How can you tell?

Drug Analyst

Drug analysts make sure that factories produce only top-quality medicine. The medicines must meet all rules set down by the government. Analysts do tests in a laboratory for the drug factories. They check that the drugs contain only the correct, pure ingredients.

To be a drug analyst for a manufacturer, you need four years of college, with courses in science. One or two years of extra training is often recommended. To learn more about being a drug analyst, write to the Food and Drug Administration, 5600 Fishers Lane, Rockville, MD 20857.

Health Career

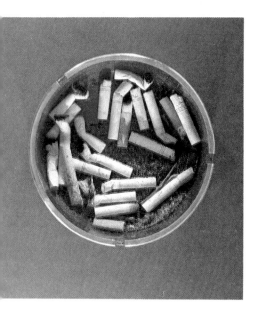

How can drugs in tobacco smoke cause damage to a smoker's heart and lungs?

Cutting Down on Cigarettes

There is an effort to get people to smoke less. Cigarette companies cannot put ads on TV or radio. Cigarette packages must have a warning on them. Restaurants often have a place for nonsmokers to sit. Many clinics try to help people who want to stop smoking.

Tobacco

Mrs. Adams was flying to Japan. She didn't want to sit near someone who might smoke. So she sat in the NO SMOKING section.

Many people smoke tobacco in the form of cigarettes, cigars, or in pipes. Tobacco smoke contains strong drugs. These drugs can be harmful to your health. They can also be harmful to nonsmokers. Cigarette smokers get the worst effects of smoking. They pull the smoke all the way into their lungs as they breathe in.

The tar and nicotine in tobacco smoke are harmful. These drugs can do great damage to a smoker's lungs and heart.

Tar is a sticky, dark substance. It can coat the air passages to the lungs. It can also coat the lungs themselves. This makes it hard for oxygen to pass into the smoker's blood. Without enough oxygen, a person becomes tired.

Nicotine can make smokers feel weak and dizzy. It can also damage the heart. Nicotine goes into the blood. It makes the openings of the blood vessels smaller than they should be. That makes it hard for blood to travel through the blood vessels. Then the body can't get the oxygen it needs. The heart must pump harder. This can overwork and weaken the smoker's heart.

Smoking may cause a very serious illness called **lung cancer.** The cells of the lungs grow out of control and lumps form. These lumps keep the lungs from working the way they should.

Why Some People Use Alcohol and Tobacco

Some people begin to smoke or drink because they are curious. They want to find out what it is like. Some young people may want to show off to their friends. They may think that smoking and drinking are signs that they are older. These are not good reasons.

Advertisements affect some people, too. In ads, happy, laughing people are often smoking and holding a drink. These people look healthy. The only drugs that can help keep people healthy are those that are needed from medicines.

Some people smoke or drink because it has become a habit. Often it is very hard for a smoker or drinker to quit. It is easier not to start smoking or drinking. Many people do not smoke or drink.

More and more people are thinking about the dangers of using harmful drugs. People can make themselves feel good in many healthful ways. They can enjoy playing and working. They can enjoy being with their families and friends. Things people do to feel good should be things that are good for them as well.

Why might people want to sit in the NO SMOKING section of a restaurant?

Talking About Advertisements

Go through some magazines or newspapers. Collect ads for cigarettes or drinks with alcohol. Discuss with your classmates how each ad tries to make its product look good.

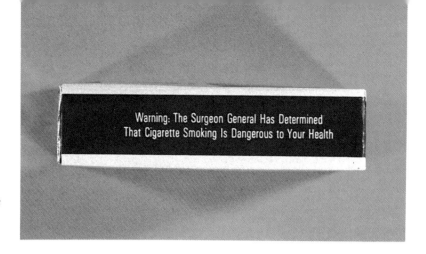

Warning: The Surgeon General Has Determined That Cigarette Smoking Is Dangerous to Your Health

What does the warning on this package of cigarettes say about the use of tobacco?

Laws About the Use of Alcohol and Tobacco

Many laws protect people from the harmful effects of alcohol and tobacco. People your age are not allowed to buy cigarettes or drinks with alcohol in them. Anyone who breaks these laws can get into serious trouble.

It is against the law for a person to drive a car if he or she has had too much alcohol to drink. If the police stop a driver, they may test that person's breath. The test shows how much alcohol it contains. Then the police will know if that person has broken the law. In some states, people can call a special number to report a driver who has had too much alcohol.

REVIEW IT NOW

1. What are some of the things caffeine can do to a person's body?
2. Why can drinking alcohol be dangerous?
3. What do tar and nicotine do to a person's heart and lungs?
4. How do laws try to protect people against the harmful effects of drugs?

Visiting a Pharmacy

Arrange for a family visit to a pharmacy. Talk with the pharmacists. Ask them to show you the equipment they use to fill the doctors' prescriptions. If they have a computer, perhaps they will show you how it works. While you are there, find out the answers to these questions:

1. What are child-guard medicine caps? Why are they used?
2. How do the pharmacists count out medicine tablets?
3. What medicine safety rules do the pharmacists suggest for homes?

To Help You Review

Checking Your Understanding

Write the numbers from 1 to 12 on your paper. After each number, write the answer to the question. Page numbers in ( ) tell you where to look in the chapter if you need help.

1. What is a drug? (**148**)
2. What are two things medicines can do? (**148**)
3. What are some things people drink that have drugs in them? (**149**)
4. How is an antibiotic drug made? (**149**)
5. How do antibiotics help fight illness? (**149**)
6. What is the difference between an OTC medicine and a prescription medicine? (**151–152**)
7. What are three reasons why medicines need to be used with care? (**152, 154**)
8. What is some of the information found on a medicine label? (**156**)
9. What are two drugs in tobacco smoke? (**157**)
10. What are some of the changes caffeine can make in the body? (**158**)
11. What are some changes alcohol can make in the body? (**158**)
12. What are two ways that laws protect people from the harmful effects of alcohol and tobacco? (**162**)

Checking Your Health Vocabulary

Write the numbers from 1 to 6 on your paper. After each number, write the letter of the meaning for the word or words. Page numbers in ( ) tell you where to look in the chapter if you need help.

1. drugs (**148**)
2. penicillin (**149**)
3. over-the-counter medicines (**151**)
4. prescription (**151**)
5. pharmacist (**151**)
6. prescription medicines (**152**)

a. a person who prepares an order from a doctor
b. medicines people can buy without a doctor's order
c. a doctor's order for a medicine
d. things other than food that can make a change in your body
e. a strong drug made from a mold
f. medicines that can only be bought with a doctor's order

Write the numbers from 7 to 13 on your paper. Then write a sentence that explains the meaning of each word or words. Page numbers in ( ) tell you where to look in the chapter if you need help.

7. antibiotic (**149**)
8. side effects (**156**)
9. caffeine (**157**)
10. alcohol (**157**)
11. tar (**157**)
12. nicotine (**157**)
13. lung cancer (**160**)

Practice Test

True or False?

Write the numbers from 1 to 15 on your paper. After each number, write *T* if the sentence is *true*. Write *F* if it is *false*. Rewrite each false sentence to make it true.

1. All drugs are medicines.
2. Medicines come in many forms.
3. How a drug is used is not important.
4. Drugs can only be found in drugstores.
5. People take antibiotics to help keep an illness from getting worse.
6. Penicillin is made from bacteria.
7. Anyone can get a job preparing medicines in a drugstore.
8. A person can only get an over-the-counter medicine with a prescription.
9. Prescription medicines must be taken for an exact length of time.
10. Medicines can lose their strength.
11. Labels on medicine tell about possible side effects.
12. Caffeine is found in milk.
13. People who have drinks with alcohol should drive only during the day.
14. Cigarette smoking can be harmful to the heart and lungs.
15. Anyone can buy cigarettes and drinks with alcohol if he or she has enough money.

Complete the Sentence

Write the numbers from 16 to 20 on your paper. After each number, copy the sentence and fill in the missing word.

16. Drugs can be both helpful and _____ to your body.
17. Strong antibiotic drugs, such as _____ , can be harmful if they aren't used carefully.
18. People should always read the _____ on a medicine before using it.
19. People who smoke _____ get the worst effects from smoking.
20. A person who has had some _____ to drink should not drive a car.

Learning More

For You to Do

1. Talk with an adult in your family. Find out if you are allergic to any medicines. Make a list of any allergies that you discover and remember them. Knowing your allergies to drugs is important in staying healthy.

2. Many people find tobacco smoke unpleasant. For this reason, buses, trains, and airplanes have NO SMOKING sections. Many restaurants and movie theaters have them, too. The next time you travel or go to a restaurant or theater, ask if there is a NO SMOKING section. You may choose to sit there and enjoy cleaner air.

3. Talk to your family about checking the medicines in your medicine cabinet. Are all the medicines out of the reach of children? Are they all clearly marked? Are any medicines too old to keep?

For You to Find Out

1. Parts of many common plants are poisonous. Use library books or an encyclopedia. Find out the poisonous part of these plants:
   - tomato
   - potato
   - cherry
   - peach
   - rhubarb

2. Hundreds of years ago American Indians discovered that chewing willow leaves took away certain pains. The leaves contained the same chemical used in aspirin today. Use library books or an encyclopedia. Find out what other medicines were discovered by chance. How were they found? Why are they useful?

For You to Read

Here are some books you can look for in your school or public library. They will help you to find out more about drugs and health.

Hyde, Margaret, and Hyde, Bruce. *Know About Drugs.* McGraw-Hill, 1979.

Terry, Luther, and Horn, Daniel. *To Smoke Or Not To Smoke.* Lothrop, 1969.

CHAPTER 8

Home, School, and Travel Safety

Accidents can happen anywhere or at any time. They can happen while you are walking down the street. Accidents can happen at home or in school. They can happen while you are traveling, too.

You can't prevent all accidents. You can find out how to prevent many of them. You can find out some of the things that make accidents happen. You can follow safety rules to avoid accidents.

You can learn the best thing to do if an accident does happen. By knowing what to do, you can keep an accident from becoming more serious.

BEING SAFE FROM ACCIDENTS

You may try to take very good care of yourself. Yet, an **accident** may happen. An accident is an unexpected event that could harm someone. Many accidents can be avoided. Learning some causes of accidents can help you learn ways to keep safe.

Being Careful

Some accidents happen because people are careless. They aren't looking out for **hazards.** A hazard is a danger. A big bump in the street is a hazard. A car or bicycle could ride over it and go out of control. At home, a toy that is left on the stairs is a hazard. Someone could fall over it. Hazards can lead to accidents.

Reggie wanted to show his friend Ernie how well he could skate backwards. Reggie skated over a large crack in the sidewalk and fell. He couldn't see the hazard. Reggie could have had a bad accident. He could have hurt others, too.

Karen was on her way to school. She stopped at the street corner in front of her house. She looked in both directions before crossing. Karen was obeying an important **safety rule.** Safety rules are rules to help keep you from harm.

Thinking Ahead of Time

Many accidents can be stopped by thinking ahead about what can happen. Peter saw that the reflector on his bicycle was broken. He wanted to ride to his friend Paul's house. Peter did not want to use broken equipment. He fixed the reflector on his

What is one reason to look out for hazards such as this?

bicycle. He thought ahead of time about what could happen.

Milt and his friends wanted to play in a vacant lot near his house. His mother said it was not safe. Some workers had left large, empty containers there. His mother told Milt never to crawl into boxes or containers. The lid could slam shut and trap him inside. Milt and his friends decided to play in the schoolyard.

Patsy is careful outside. She thinks about what can happen. She goes slowly down her driveway on her bicycle. Patsy stops when she gets to the road. She is watching out for people on the sidewalk. She also looks in both directions to see if there are any cars coming.

Patsy watches out for the bump at the end of her street. She pays attention to special signs, too. When she sees DANGER—WORKERS, she rides along the other side of the street.

Discussing Safety in the Playground

Accidents can happen in the playground. They can happen even when the equipment is in good condition. Think about the things you find in a playground. Then think about how they could cause accidents. Discuss with your classmates how these accidents may be avoided.

How is Peter thinking ahead of time to help prevent accidents?

What limit has this family set? What other limits might the family set?

Obeying Limits

As you grow older, you can do more things on your own. But there are still some things you can't do alone. Your family must set a **limit.** This is the point at which you must stop. It is the farthest you should go when you are doing something.

Think about the limits set by your family. Sometimes families limit use of the stove to a time when adults are there.

You may have limits outdoors, too. Maybe you can go only so far from home. Perhaps you have to come right home after school. How can these limits help keep you safe?

Discussing Limits

Discuss limits with your classmates and family. What are some good limits at home? Name some good limits in school and outdoors.

REVIEW IT NOW

1. What is a hazard?
2. What are safety rules?
3. What are three important things you can do to be safe from accidents?

Robots

Robots are machines that can do work for people. Some robots look like people. Some move like people. Others don't look like humans at all.

Many companies use robots to improve safety conditions in their factories. Instead of having a person do a dangerous job, they use a robot. For example, many parts of cars are welded together. Welding is heating pieces of metal and joining them together. Welding can cause terrible burns on humans. A robot feels no pain. It can do the job safely and quickly.

Health Today

SAFETY AT HOME

Beth and her father built a treehouse in their yard. Beth's father let her do the jobs she could safely handle. He cut the wood with a power saw. Beth nailed pieces of wood together. He also attached the treehouse to the strong lower branches of the tree. Finally, the house was finished. Beth's father showed her how to use the short ladder to climb safely to and from her treehouse.

Preventing Accidents at Home

Beth and her father followed safety rules when they built the treehouse. Following safety rules can help prevent accidents at home.

Beth's mother and father had set down safety rules. For example, Beth had to pick up her toys when she was finished playing with them. Toys that are left lying around can be hazards. If any of her toys broke, she or an adult fixed them.

In what ways did Beth and her father follow safety rules when building the treehouse?

Beth's father and mother had a workshop in the garage. They kept paint, cleaning materials, and gasoline there. These materials contain poisons. Beth helped her father label these things. That way Beth knew these were harmful materials.

Beth knows how to avoid electric shocks, too. She does not use power tools without help from her father or mother. Beth also watches for any worn-out electric wires around the house. People in the family know they should not touch anything electric with wet hands.

Knowing What to Do

Mickey's mother went to visit a neighbor. Mrs. Berlin left the neighbor's phone number for Mickey. He and his brother Danny were playing. Suddenly, Danny caught his finger in a door. Mickey stayed calm. He gave Danny some ice wrapped in a towel to hold on his finger. Then he called his mother. Mickey had known just what to do. He had stayed calm. He had called an adult.

How do the labels shown help prevent accidents at home?

Warnings on Poisons

The FDA (Food and Drug Administration) is part of the United States government. The FDA has made some laws for your safety. One of these laws states that containers with poisons inside must have a warning on them. Words like "Caution" or "Danger" let you know that whatever is inside is a hazard. Labels tell what to do if the material is swallowed. They also tell what to do if the material gets in someone's eyes or on someone's skin.

Mickey had acted quickly in an **emergency.** An emergency is a sudden need that calls for immediate help. One big home emergency is a fire. Knowing what to do can save people's lives.

If you smell smoke or see flames, stay calm. Shout "Fire!" Leave your house as soon as you can. Tell a neighbor to call the fire department. Or, pull the nearest fire alarm you can find.

You might be in your room with the door closed. You may see smoke coming through the cracks. Again, shout "Fire!" as loud as you can. Your door may feel hot. That means the fire is nearby. Opening a door if there is a fire outside is dangerous. Block the cracks with towels or clothing. Open a window and climb out if you can safely do so.

You might have to go through heavy smoke. Stay close to the floor. Cover your mouth and nose with a cloth or piece of clothing. Don't breathe deeply.

Why should people have smoke alarms and fire extinguishers in their homes?

REVIEW IT NOW

1. What are four ways to avoid accidents in your home?
2. What are two important things you should do in case of an emergency?
3. What could you do if you woke up to find smoke coming under the door of your room?

Sue August

Sue August is never very far from her signal box. Sue is captain of the ambulance drivers in Franklin Lakes, New Jersey. When the signal sounds, Sue rushes to her ambulance. Sometimes she drives people to the hospital. Often, she cares for them on the way there.

Sue knows how to treat many emergencies. She can put a splint on a broken bone. A splint is something that holds a broken bone together. Sue can also help people who have had heart attacks. As captain, she chooses new ambulances and lifesaving equipment, too.

Sue often visits schools to teach about health and safety.

Focus On

What are two important rules to follow when there is a fire drill at school?

SAFETY AWAY FROM HOME

Accidents sometimes happen when you are away from home. As you get older, you do more kinds of things. There are more chances for accidents to happen. It is important to obey safety rules when you are away from home. If you do, you will probably be safe even if you are trying something new.

Being Safe at School

Julio is a safety monitor. He likes helping other children to be safe at school. Julio makes sure the children don't walk too fast or run through the halls. He sees that they don't run down the stairs. Julio stops children who push at the drinking fountain.

Julio also knows it is important to pay attention during fire drills. Julio and his classmates become quiet when they hear the fire signal for the drill. They listen to the teacher's instructions. The teacher gives them information that will help them be safe.

Making a School Safety Chart

Get together with your classmates. Find out from the adults in your school all the school safety rules. Include safety in the gym, the lunchroom, and the schoolyard. Make a large safety chart for everyone to see and discuss. Post the chart in the classroom.

178

Being Safe Outdoors

It was Safety Week in school. Mr. Gordon's class talked about keeping safe. One of the things they talked about was outdoor safety.

Kara said that she is careful when she plays with outdoor equipment. She once got hit in the leg by a baseball bat that someone threw. Louise said she hurt her knees and elbows a lot when she was learning to roller skate. Now, she wears pads while she practices roller skating.

Mario told how important it is to pay attention to signs. He watched an old brick building being torn down. One brick just missed hitting someone. That person ignored a DANGER sign. Anita said a friend once dared her to walk across a narrow railroad bridge. Anita said she wouldn't do it.

How is Louise helping to keep herself safe outdoors?

What outdoor safety tip is this boy following?

Mr. Gordon's class made an Outdoor Safety poster. This is what it said.

Outdoor Safety Tips

- Play only where it is safe.
- Use equipment correctly.
- Use masks and pads when you need protection during a game.
- Pay attention to warning signs.
- Don't take foolish chances.
- Stay away from places that might be dangerous.

Being Safe in the Water

Another thing Mr. Gordon's class talked about was water safety. They all agreed it is important to know the safety rules before going near the water.

Heather told the class how she followed the rules for water safety. Heather went swimming often during her vacation. She went to pools, lakes, and beaches.

Heather went in the water with a friend. She swam only where a lifeguard could see her. She never went in water that was very deep or too rough. If Heather felt cold or tired, she came right out of the water.

Sometimes, Heather's parents took her out in a rowboat. She and her parents wore life jackets. Then they would be safe if something happened and they fell into the water.

Mr. Gordon asked Heather to write down some water safety tips for the whole class to read. Here is her list.

- Swim only near a lifeguard or an adult.
- Swim with someone else.
- Only swim as far as you know you can.
- Swim only in safe water.
- Shout for help only when you mean it.
- Play carefully when you are around a pool.

Being Safe When You Travel

You spend a lot of time getting from one place to another. Sometimes you walk. Other times you ride. It is important to follow travel safety rules whenever you walk or ride.

Safety in Cars

You may often be a **passenger** in a car. Passengers ride along with a driver. The driver has the important job of driving safely. The passengers have jobs, too. They can help keep themselves safe.

Boat Safety Tips

- Wear a life jacket.
- Make sure the boat has no leaks.
- Go boating only in good weather.
- Stay still in the boat.
- If your boat turns over, hold on to it.
- Always go with an adult.

Is it safe to swim in this water? How can you tell?

How can a person be safe when getting off a bus?

Andre and his sister, Celeste, went to the store in a car with their mother. They all put on their seat belts. Before the car started up, Celeste locked all the doors. Once the car began moving, the children did not put their hands outside the windows.

Andre and Celeste were quiet in the car. They didn't want to bother their mother while she was driving. When they stopped, Mrs. Emery parked at the curb. Everyone got out on the side away from traffic.

Safety in Buses

Monica rode the yellow school bus home. Jack rode the city bus. Each one followed the safety rules for riding in buses. Monica and Jack waited in a safe place until their buses came. They both stayed in their own seats until it was time to get off the bus. They waited until the bus had stopped moving.

When Monica got off, she stepped onto the sidewalk in front of her house. Jack had to cross the street. He walked to the nearest sidewalk. Then, he waited for a green light before he crossed at a corner.

Seat Belt Safety
When a car crashes, people can be thrown at a very high speed. Adults can't act like seat belts. Holding a child on a lap won't help. Instead, both adult and child may be thrown forward if there is an accident. Everyone in a car should get in the habit of wearing a seat belt. Babies and young children should be placed in car seats.

Emergency Room Nurse

For quick emergency care, go to a hospital emergency room. Usually the first person to help is an *emergency room nurse.* A nurse checks a patient's breathing and heartbeat. An emergency room nurse also checks for broken bones and bleeding. He or she takes temperatures, cleans wounds, and gives certain medicines.

To become an emergency room nurse, you need two to four years of college. About two years of on-the-job experience usually follows. To learn more about being an emergency room nurse, write to the Emergency Department Nurses Association, 666 North Lake Shore Drive, Chicago, IL 60611.

Health Career

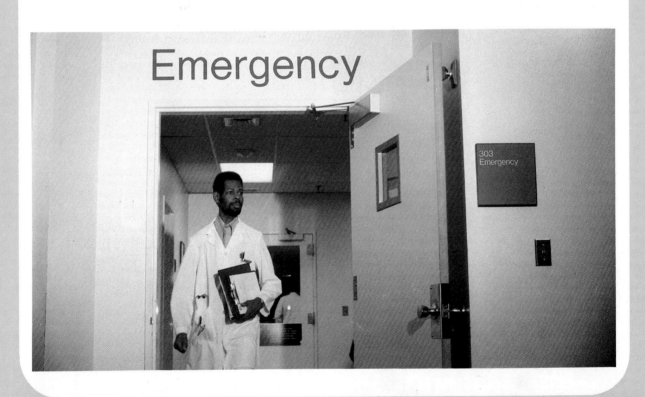

Deciding on the Safest Route

What is the safest way to walk somewhere? Often, the safest route is the one with the most traffic signals, police, or crossing guards. These people can help protect you from traffic. Where do you walk without an adult? Describe your route. How do you keep yourself safe as you walk?

What two pedestrian safety rules are these children following?

Amy is walking home from school. She is a **pedestrian,** or a person who is walking. Amy follows safety rules as she goes. She walks on the sidewalk when she can. Otherwise, she walks way over on the side of the road.

Amy crosses only when she reaches a corner. A School Crossing Guard stands on the wide street near school. Amy waits for the guard to tell her when to cross. Amy watches for cars as she crosses.

At the next corner, there is a traffic light. Amy waits until the light flashes its green WALK sign. Then she knows she can cross. Again, she watches out for cars as she walks to the other side.

Amy also knows that if she ever has to walk along the road at night, she must carry a flashlight. She would wear light colors so the drivers could see her. She would also walk on the left side of the road. That way, she can see the traffic coming toward her.

Safety on a Bicycle

When you ride your bicycle, you are the driver. If you have a bicycle, it is important for you to know bicycle safety rules.

Manuel and Kay are going for a ride on their bicycles. Manuel puts his books in a basket. Kay carries hers in a backpack. They keep both hands free for steering, except when they signal for a turn.

The children follow traffic rules for bicycle safety. They ride single file on the right side of the road. They ride in the same direction as traffic.

What bicycle safety rules are Manuel and Kay following?

Bicycle Safety Tips
• Have an adult check to see if your bicycle is the right size for you.
• Make sure the brakes, tires, and other bicycle parts are in good condition.
• Make sure your bicycle has a bell or horn. Make sure it has head and tail lights. Make sure it has reflectors on the sides and in the back, too.
• Obey all traffic rules.
• Watch out for hazards.
• Wear light clothing at night.
• Ride slowly if you are caught in the rain.

This girl is using bicycle hand signals. Which picture shows a signal for turning left? Turning right? Stopping?

Hand Signals

Right turn: Bend your left arm up.
Left turn: Hold your left arm straight out.
Stop: Bend your left arm down.

Manuel and Kay stop at the red light, just as cars do. They obey all traffic lights and stop signs. Both children obey other traffic rules, too. They slow down at crossings. When they turn, they use hand signals. They walk their bicycles across busy streets at crosswalks. They watch out for pedestrians.

Manuel and Kay watch for road hazards. They look out for holes in the road and for driveways. They also watch carefully for parked cars that might start up and pull out. When Manuel and Kay ride at night, they wear light clothing. They do this so they can be seen by drivers of cars. They also use their bicycle lights.

REVIEW IT NOW

1. What are three things to do to avoid accidents in school?
2. What are six outdoor safety tips?
3. What are some traffic rules bicycle riders should follow?

Making an Emergency Telephone List

Whom would you call in an emergency? Keeping a list of telephone numbers to call in case of injury or fire is important. Make a list like the one below. Ask an adult to help you find the telephone numbers. Fill them in and keep them near a telephone in your home. Discuss which number to call in different emergencies.

Know what to say when making an emergency call. Be prepared to tell these facts clearly:

1. What emergency has happened.
2. Your full name.
3. Your complete address.
4. Your telephone number.

You may never need to call these numbers. But knowing what to do in case you need to call them should make you feel safer.

EMERGENCY TELEPHONE NUMBERS
POLICE DEPARTMENT
FIRE DEPARTMENT
DOCTOR
POISON CONTROL CENTER
NEIGHBOR
PARENTS' WORK NUMBERS
CLOSE RELATIVE
AMBULANCE

To Help You Review

Checking Your Understanding

Write the numbers from 1 to 13 on your paper. After each number, write the answer to the question. Page numbers in ( ) tell you where to look in the chapter if you need help.

1. What is an example of a hazard you should avoid? **(170)**
2. How do safety rules help keep you from harm? **(170)**
3. What is one way that broken equipment can lead to an accident? **(170-171)**
4. What are some limits that families can set? **(172)**
5. What are three ways to be safe in your home? **(174-175)**
6. What two things can you do in case of emergencies? **(175-176)**
7. What four things should you do if there is a fire in your home? **(176)**
8. What are three safety rules to obey when you are in school? **(178)**
9. What are three outdoor safety tips that you have followed? **(180)**
10. What are three tips for water safety? **(181)**
11. What are three important safety rules to obey when you ride in a car? **(182)**
12. What are three different ways to avoid an accident when you are walking? **(184)**
13. What are three road hazards bicycle riders should watch out for? **(186)**

Checking Your Health Vocabulary

Write the numbers from 1 to 7 on your paper. After each number, write the letter of the meaning for the word or words. Page numbers in ( ) tell you where to look in the chapter if you need help.

1. accident (**170**)   **5.** emergency (**176**)
2. hazards (**170**)   **6.** passenger (**181**)
3. safety rules (**170**)   **7.** pedestrian (**184**)
4. limit (**172**)

a. a person who is walking
b. rules that help keep people from harm
c. a sudden need that calls for immediate help
d. an unexpected event that can harm someone
e. a person who rides along with the driver
f. dangers
g. the point at which a person must stop

Write the numbers from 8 to 11 on your paper. After each number, write the word or words that correctly complete each sentence in the paragraph below. Use some of the words from the vocabulary list above.

Charlie had a new bike. He didn't want to have an __(8)__ . He was careful to follow _____(9)_____ . He watched out for any __(10)__ that might make bicycle riding dangerous. He also looked out for a __(11)__ who might be walking across the street.

Practice Test

True or False?

Write the numbers from 1 to 15 on your paper. After each number, write *T* if the sentence is *true*. Write *F* if it is *false*. Rewrite each false statement to make it true.

1. Accidents can always be avoided.
2. Many accidents can be avoided.
3. Use broken equipment if you have nothing else to play with.
4. Steering with one hand while you are riding your bicycle is a good way to have fun.
5. If you hurry, you won't have time to have an accident.
6. Stoves can be dangerous.
7. The main thing to do in an emergency is to try to handle it yourself.
8. In case of fire, shouting will only scare people.
9. Teachers often have important safety information for you.
10. Wearing masks and pads when you play games won't help keep you safe.
11. It is foolish to do things just because someone dares you to do them.
12. It is wise to stay away from places that look dangerous.
13. Seat belts don't protect people in a car accident.
14. There are no special safety rules for riding in buses.
15. The main danger to pedestrians is crosswalks.

Complete the Sentence

Write the numbers from 16 to 20 on your paper. After each number, copy the sentence and fill in the missing word or words.

16. When you and a friend ride your bicycles, you should ride _____ _____ .
17. At busy crossings, a bicycle rider _____ his or her bicycle across the street.
18. For night riding or walking, wear _____ colors.
19. If you walk on the road at night, walk on the _____ side.
20. Bicycle riders should ride in the _____ direction as cars and buses.

Learning More

For You to Do

1. Make a safety check of your home. Are toys stored where people won't fall over them? Are there broken toys with sharp edges? Are there any worn-out electrical cords? Are there materials that should be labeled? Work with an adult to correct any dangers.

2. Spend a few days checking your neighborhood for warning and safety signs. Write down the information about each sign you find. Draw the signs. Talk with your family about what you have found.

3. Plan and practice a fire drill at home with your family. Make sure everyone knows what to do and how to get out quickly. After the drill, discuss what went well during the drill. Then decide what improvements you could make.

For You to Find Out

1. Find out about programs where you live that teach safety and emergency care. Talk with your local Red Cross or the Girl or Boy Scouts. They may offer a class that interests you.

2. Think about what you would do in each emergency below. Then talk with an adult or look in a library book. Find out if your thinking was correct.
   - You are locked out of your house.
   - Your little sister fell out of a tree. Her leg might be broken.
   - There is a fire in your room.

For You to Read

Here are some books you can look for in your school or public library. They will help you to find out more about safety and emergency care.

Vandenburg, Mary Lou. *Help! Emergencies That Could Happen to You and How to Handle Them.* Minneapolis: Lerner, 1975.

Witty, Margot. *A Day in the Life of an Emergency Room Nurse.* Mahwah, N.J.: Troll Associates, 1980.

CHAPTER 9

Your Health and Your Community

People want to live where it is safe and healthy. There are workers whose jobs are to make a place safe and healthy. There are rules and laws to protect everyone's health and safety, too.

There are many things you can do to help make your town or city a safe and healthy place to live.

WHAT IS A COMMUNITY?

A **community** is a place where people live, work, play, and go to school. It is also a place where people get many of the things they need for a happy and healthy life.

A community can be any size. It can be a large city. It can be a small town or a suburb. People living in the same community need one another for many things.

Communities Can Be Different

Communities are not all alike. Buddy lives in a house in the country. The houses in Buddy's community are far apart from one another. People don't have sidewalks near their homes. Buddy uses main roads and side roads to get places.

Look at the communities on pages 194 and 195. How are they different? In what ways might they be alike?

Craig lives in a house on a block with many other houses. Craig's community is made up of many blocks very much like his.

Angela lives in an apartment building in a city. More than 20 families live in her building. The city where Angela lives has many apartment houses like Angela's. It has many homes, too.

Communities Can Be Alike

Do you live in the country or in a small town? Do you live in a city or a suburb? Wherever you live, you probably are not too far from schools, stores, and offices. You are probably fairly close to a hospital. Most likely, there is a fire station and a police station near you, too. All of these buildings are for everyone in your community to use.

What are some things people in a community share?

People in a community share more than buildings. They may get their food and water from the same places. They breathe the same air. People in a community share the same streets.

For these reasons, people in a community need laws to help keep them safe and healthy. They need laws to make sure their food and water are clean. People in a community need laws to help them keep the air and streets clean and safe. People in a community also need special groups of workers to help keep them safe and healthy.

REVIEW IT NOW

1. What is a community?
2. What are three ways in which communities can be different?
3. What are five important things people in a community share?

COMMUNITY HEALTH TEAMS

Each community has people who work for people's safety and health. You have probably met some of these workers. You will be reading about others for the first time.

Safety Workers

Every community has **safety workers.** Safety workers are people who try to keep other people safe.

Firefighters

Some safety workers are firefighters. You have probably seen fire trucks rushing to a fire. Firefighters put out fires. They try to save people trapped in burning buildings. Firefighters also try to keep fires from spreading.

Some firefighters inspect buildings. Mr. Haskins is a fire inspector. He checks buildings to see if they are safe. He makes sure fire alarms and sprinklers are working. He looks for hazards such as uncovered wires and open cans of liquids that can burn easily.

Early Firefighters

Long ago, people didn't have fire trucks or modern equipment. When a fire broke out, people had to use buckets of water. Many people would form a line. Each person would pass buckets of water to the people at the fire. Then the people nearest the fire would pass the empty buckets back along the line to be filled up again. Think about how fires are put out today. Which way do you think works better? Why?

In what way is Officer Murray helping to keep people in the community safe?

Helping in Police Work

Some communities have specially trained police dogs. Trained dogs help the police to find criminals. The dogs can help in other ways, too. These dogs are part of the Canine Corps. *Canine* means "dog." Do you know if your community has a Canine Corps? How can you find out?

Police Officers

Officer Murray is a police officer. She does different jobs at different times. Officer Murray controls crowds when there is a big parade. Sometimes, she controls traffic, too. Officer Murray makes sure that drivers stay within speed limits.

Sometimes Officer Murray walks or drives around a neighborhood. She checks to see that everything is all right. She can often tell when something looks wrong. Officer Murray may be able to stop a crime from happening.

Officer Murray gives people safety tips. She teaches children bicycle safety. She tells adults how to keep their homes safe. Often, she helps children who can't find their way home. Officer Murray sometimes helps people who are hurt or ill.

Firefighter

Firefighters must be ready to help a community in many emergencies. They must know what kind of fire is burning and how to put it out. Firefighters learn the safest way of finding and rescuing people. They treat people who are burned or who are ill from breathing too much smoke.

Someone who wants to become a firefighter usually needs four years of high school. He or she often trains at a fire academy for six weeks to six months. To learn more about being a firefighter, write to the National Fire Protection Association, 60 Batterymarch Street, Boston, MA 02110.

Health
Career

Other Safety Workers

Mrs. Lefkowitz is a safety worker. She is a school crossing guard. Her job is to protect children when they cross wide streets near their school. She uses her hands to signal when it is safe to cross. She can also use her hands to signal to cars when they must wait.

Mr. Chesney is a sanitation worker. One of his jobs is to collect garbage and trash. Sanitation workers help keep the streets clean by sweeping and washing them, too. Some sanitation workers make streets and roads safe for travel. They may clear away snow and ice. They also clear away broken glass or leaves, which can cause accidents. In some towns, sanitation workers spread salt or sand on slippery roads.

These community workers are cutting branches away from electric lines. How does this help to keep a community safe?

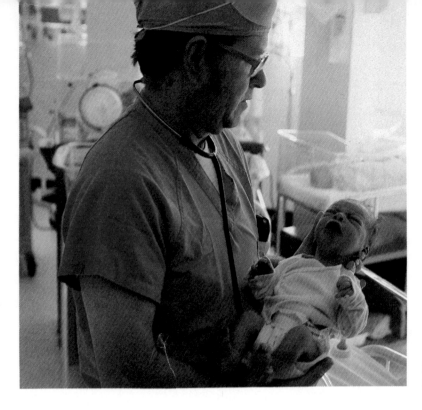

What kind of health worker is taking care of this baby?

Health Workers

Every community has **health workers.** These are workers who try to keep people healthy.

Doctors, Dental Hygienists, and Public Health Nurses

Dr. Avery treats only children. Doctors who treat only children are called pediatricians. Dr. Avery begins every day in the hospital. He may visit some children who are ill. He sees how newborn babies are doing. Then, he helps children in his office.

Ms. Fisher is a dental hygienist. She examines people's teeth. Ms. Fisher also cleans teeth. She teaches people how to care for their teeth and gums.

Mr. Webster is a public health nurse. He works for the community's public health office. His job takes him to many places. Today, Mr. Webster is visiting a mother and her newborn baby. He will examine the baby. Mr. Webster will also help the mother to learn how to take good care of her baby.

Learning About Community Health Educators

Many communities have community health educators. These workers plan programs for schools or for groups of people in the community. They help people learn ways to be healthy. They may teach things such as correct dental care and healthful ways to eat and exercise.

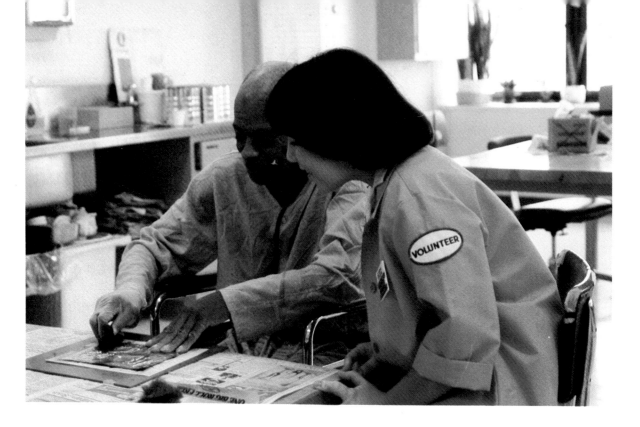

What kinds of jobs can a hospital volunteer do to help people?

Recreation Therapists and Dietitians

Mrs. Franklin is a recreation therapist. She plans activities such as games and dancing for people who are in the hospital. Recreation therapists believe that people who are ill may get well sooner if they are busy and having a good time.

Mr. Hale works in a hospital, too. He is a dietitian. One of his jobs is to plan the meals for the patients. Mr. Hale must be sure that the patients get balanced diets. He must also try to plan meals that all the different patients will enjoy.

Hospital Volunteers and Laboratory Technicians

Ms. Armstrong is a hospital **volunteer.** A volunteer is a person who works without pay. Ms. Armstrong spends a few hours every week helping people in the hospital. She does many kinds of jobs.

Sometimes she works in the hospital gift shop. Often, she helps the nurses. For example, she may take new patients to their rooms.

Mr. Hartman is a laboratory technician. He works in a special place in the hospital called a laboratory. There, he may examine someone's blood under a microscope. He looks to see if it is healthy. Mr. Hartman may also look at germs from a person's throat. He finds out what kind of germs they are. Then he sends his report to a doctor. The report will help the doctor treat a person who is ill.

Inspectors

Mrs. Santos is a food inspector. She goes to restaurants and other places where food is prepared. Mrs. Santos checks to see that the food is safe for people to eat. She makes sure the places where the food is kept are clean. She knows that food can carry germs that can make people ill. Mrs. Santos makes sure there are places for the workers to wash their hands. Mrs. Santos may find a place that is not clean. Then she makes out a report. A place that isn't clean can be closed by a community's health department.

Water inspectors are another kind of health worker. They go to a community's water supply. The inspectors get samples of water. They test the samples to see if they are free of germs that may cause illness. Harmful material in rivers, lakes, and oceans is called **water pollution.** Chemicals, trash, and other wastes can **pollute,** or harm, water. Polluted water often has harmful germs. Many communities have laws to help stop water pollution.

How can water pollution harm people's health?

Being a Health Inspector

Who are some of the people around you who handle food for many people every day? Think about people in schools, restaurants, and supermarkets. Interview one of these persons. Find out some of the things that are done to help keep your food clean and safe to eat.

What are some things that may cause air pollution?

Some health workers test the air around us. The air we breathe affects our health. Fumes from cars and factories may cause **air pollution.** Air pollution is dirt and other materials that are harmful to breathe. Smoke and dust can cause air pollution.

People who check the air test it to see if it is clean enough to breathe. They report what they find. Sometimes the air is not safe to breathe.

REVIEW IT NOW

1. What do safety workers do to help people in a community?
2. What do health workers do to help people in a community?
3. What can cause water pollution?
4. What is air pollution?

Tel-Med

Many communities offer instant health facts. Callers phone a special number at a hospital to reach *Tel-Med.* They tell Tel-Med what they want to know about health care. A child might call Tel-Med to find out what it is like to go to a hospital. A tape recording would tell all about what it is like to be in a hospital.

The recordings are clear and easy to understand. Some students call Tel-Med for help with school reports. Experts at the hospital check that all the facts on the tape recordings are correct. Tel-Med should not replace a doctor or other health worker.

Health Today

HELPING YOUR COMMUNITY

People in communities share many important things. Sometimes people can do things to harm the health of others in their community. Communities have ways to help keep people safe and healthy. You can help keep your community safe and healthy.

Keeping Air and Water Clean

Most communities have laws to help keep air and water clean. People can't put wastes into lakes and rivers. There are also laws to keep smoke and harmful fumes out of the air. In some communities, smoking tobacco in certain places is not allowed. You may have seen NO SMOKING signs in elevators or in restaurants.

Keeping Streets and Sidewalks Clean

Dropping trash on the ground is called **littering.** Camilla is walking down the street. She has just finished her small bag of nuts. She looks for a trash basket. When she finds one, she drops in the bag. Camilla knows that trash on the sidewalk makes a community look ugly.

How can people in a community help keep their sidewalks and streets clean?

Harry is walking his dog, Blackie. He makes sure that Blackie doesn't dirty the street. Dog and cat wastes contain harmful germs. Many communities have strict laws about such wastes. They say that pet owners must clean up after their animals.

How is Harry helping to keep his community clean?

Following Other Community Health Laws

Too much noise is unhealthy. It can disturb people's work and rest. Loud noise can cause people's hearts to beat faster. It may even cause hearing loss. Car horns can make too much noise. Machines and radios can be too loud. All these noises are called **noise pollution.** Many communities have laws against noise pollution.

Many communities have health rules about how you use public places. Penny often goes to the public pool. She must shower before she goes into the pool.

Finding Out About Pollution Laws

What laws does your community have about littering? What laws does it have about noise pollution? Try to find out.

207

How can recycling metal, glass, and newspapers help a community?

Recycling

Neal collects cans, bottles, and newspapers. He has learned that these things can be reused. Neal takes these things to a **recycling center.** The center can recycle, or use these things again.

Getting rid of trash and garbage can be a problem. Burning garbage and trash can pollute the air. In some places, it is against the law to burn trash and garbage. Some communities bury their trash. Others recycle many kinds of trash. Metal cans can be melted down to be used again. Paper can be made into new paper. Glass can be reused, too.

Neal is helping to recycle trash in his community. He is helping to cut down on the amount of trash that needs to be thrown away. He is helping to make his community a better place to live.

Deciding What You Can Do

What can you and your classmates do to help your community? Plan some projects. Work together to decide how you can carry out these projects.

Elaine Valois

Elaine Valois is well known in Toledo, Ohio, for her work in recycling. Elaine recycles all the newspapers, cardboard, magazines, glass, and metal containers she uses. Elaine separates each kind of material. Then she takes it to recycling centers in her community.

Elaine's vegetable garden is one of the best around. She mixes her vegetable peelings with soil. This mixture makes the soil very rich.

Elaine believes we must not throw away materials that can be used again. She teaches others how to buy products that can be recycled.

Focus On

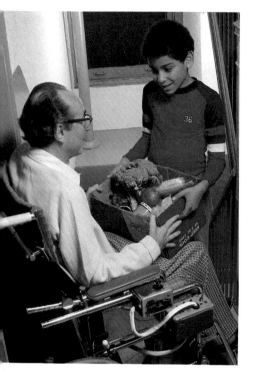

Neal and his friends do other things to help their community. One week, they helped clean up a park that was filled with litter. They went to the park early in the day. All the children had large plastic bags for the litter. By late afternoon, all the litter had been picked up.

Another time, Neal and his friends gathered up all their old toys. Neal's parents fixed the ones that were broken. The children took their toys to a nearby children's hospital.

Neal's neighbor, Mr. Porter, can't get around very much. Sometimes, Neal goes to the store for him. Other times, Neal just visits with Mr. Porter. Mr. Porter saves all his old cans and newspapers for Neal's recycling project.

What are some ways that Neal and his friends help their community? What might you and your friends do to help your community?

REVIEW IT NOW

1. What three health rules help protect people in a community?
2. How can people avoid littering?
3. What causes noise pollution?
4. Why is it important for a community to have a recycling center?

Visiting a Police Station

Telephone the police station in your community. Tell your name and age. Explain that you would like to visit the station. Ask an adult to go with you. Set a day for the visit.

When you go to the station, find out the answers to these questions:

1. What different jobs do the police do for the community?
2. What kind of emergency calls do they get?
3. What safety facts do the police tell people in the community?
4. What special equipment helps the police protect the community?

Beyond the Classroom

To Help You Review

Checking Your Understanding

Write the numbers from 1 to 12 on your paper. After each number, write the answer to the question. Page numbers in ( ) tell you where to look in the chapter if you need help.

1. What are three kinds of communities? **(194-195)**
2. What are two ways that community rules help keep people healthy and safe? **(196)**
3. How does a fire inspector try to prevent fires? **(197)**
4. How does a police officer help keep people safe? **(198)**
5. How does a sanitation worker make streets safe for travel? **(200)**
6. What is one thing a dietitian does? **(202)**
7. What are two things a laboratory technician does? **(203)**
8. What does a food inspector do in a restaurant? **(203)**
9. How does a health worker help to keep air clean? **(204)**
10. What are two laws that help protect people against tobacco smoke and litter? **(206-207)**
11. What is noise pollution? **(207)**
12. What kinds of trash can be recycled at a recycling center? **(208)**

Checking Your Health Vocabulary

Write the numbers from 1 to 5 on your paper. After each number, write the letter of the meaning for the word or words. Page numbers in ( ) tell you where to look in the chapter if you need help.

1. community (**194**)   **4.** volunteer (**202**)
2. safety workers (**197**)   **5.** water pollution (**203**)
3. health workers (**201**)

a. workers who try to keep people healthy
b. workers who help keep people free from harm
c. someone who works without pay
d. place where people live, work, and play
e. harmful material in rivers, lakes, and oceans

Write the numbers from 6 to 9 on your paper. Then write a sentence that explains the meaning of each word or words. Page numbers in ( ) tell you where to look in the chapter if you need help.

6. air pollution (**204**)   **8.** noise pollution (**207**)
7. littering (**206**)   **9.** recycling center (**208**)

Practice Test

True or False?

Write the numbers from 1 to 15 on your paper. After each number, write *T* if the sentence is *true*. Write *F* if it is *false*. Rewrite each false sentence to make it true.

1. All communities are alike.
2. Some firefighters check out buildings for hazards.
3. Police departments only do the job of catching people who break the law.
4. A school crossing guard helps children cross streets safely.
5. Sanitation workers only collect garbage and trash.
6. A pediatrician is a doctor who takes care of children.
7. Public health nurses always work in one place.
8. A recreation therapist exercises people's muscles.
9. A dietitian is in charge of keeping a hospital clean.
10. A volunteer gets paid for the work he or she does.
11. A laboratory technician looks at someone's blood under a microscope.
12. A food inspector checks to see if food in restaurants is tasty.
13. A water inspector inspects water for germs.
14. Noise pollution is caused by sound that is too loud.
15. Some trash can be recycled.

Complete the Sentence

Write the numbers from 16 to 20 on your paper. After each number, copy the sentence and fill in the missing word or words.

16. People in a _____ share many things.
17. It is important that the _____ people breathe be clean.
18. Public places often help fight air pollution by putting up _____ _____ signs.
19. People's work and _____ can be disturbed by noise pollution.
20. Glass, _____, and _____ can be made useful again by recycling.

Learning More

For You to Do

1. Look around your neighborhood. Is it clean and neat? Are there papers and garbage around? Use a plastic garbage bag. Collect any litter you see near your home. Ask an adult to help you. Help make your neighborhood a cleaner place.

2. Visit a fire station. Talk with the person in charge. Discuss the different kinds of fires. Ask what firefighters use to put out each kind. Ask to see the equipment that helps firefighters do their jobs.

3. Read all the traffic signs you see. Make sure you understand what each one means. If you have any questions, ask an adult.

For You to Find Out

1. What happens to garbage after trash collectors take it away? Is any of it used to help people? Where does the rest of it go? Look in a library book or an encyclopedia. You might talk with a trash collector. Find out the answers.

2. Many communities must treat their water before it is clean enough for people to drink. Use an encyclopedia. Find out how water is cleaned.

3. What laws must restaurants obey in your community? Talk with a restaurant owner or worker. Find out about laws that help keep food and eating places clean.

For You to Read

Here are some books you can look for in your school or public library. They will help you to find out more about community health.

Beame, Rona. *What Happens to Garbage?* Messner, 1978.

Howe, James. *The Hospital Book.* Crown, 1981.

Smith, Betsy. *A Day in the Life of a Firefighter.* Mahwah, N.J.: Troll Associates, 1981.

EXERCISE HANDBOOK

This special part of your health book is about exercise. It shows you exercises that are fun and easy to do. These exercises can help you feel good and look good. They can help you lose weight. They can help your heart and lungs work well. And they can help you relax.

The Exercise Handbook is divided into four parts: "Stretching Out," "Individual Exercise," "Group Exercise," and "Cooling Down."

You should exercise at least every other day for 15 minutes or more. Exercising in this way can help keep you healthy now and throughout your life. Before you begin your exercise program, be sure to check with your doctor. Some exercises may not be safe for you. Your doctor can decide which exercises you should do and which ones you should not do.

STRETCHING OUT

Every time you exercise, begin by stretching out the muscles of your body. Stretching out your muscles helps keep them from being hurt when you exercise hard. Here are some stretching exercises you can do before playing a game or sport. Each of these exercises stretches a different group of muscles. You should do several exercises each time you stretch out. This way you will stretch different groups of muscles.

Head Rolls

1. Stand with your legs slightly apart. Keep your arms at your sides.

2. Gently roll your head in a circle as shown in picture 1. As you roll your head forward, try to touch your chest with your chin.

3. Repeat step 2. This time roll your head in the opposite direction.

4. Repeat steps 2 and 3 in order four times.

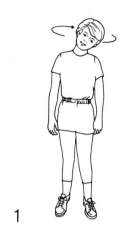

1

Spinal Twist

1. Stand with your feet about as far apart as your shoulders. Stand as straight as you can.

2. Hold your arms straight out at each side. Keep them as high as your shoulders.

3. Gently twist your body and arms from side to side as shown in picture 2. Make sure your head and body go in the same direction. Keep your feet in one place as you twist.

4. Repeat step 3 four times.

2

Chest and Upper-Back Stretch

1. Stand with your feet as far apart as your shoulders. Clasp your hands behind your back.

2. Lean your head toward the floor. Bend at the waist. Keep your knees and arms straight.

3. As you bend forward, point your arms toward the ceiling as shown in picture 3. Breathe in as you bend forward.

3

4. Return to the position in step 1. Breathe out as you straighten up.

5. Repeat steps 2 and 3 four times.

Calf Stretch

1. Stand with your hips facing straight ahead.

2. Put your right leg forward. Put your left leg back.

3. Keep your heels on the ground. Keep your left leg straight. Bend your right leg as shown in picture 4. You should feel a stretch in your left calf.

4

4. Return to the position in step 1. Repeat steps 2 and 3. This time bend your left leg. Keep your right leg straight.

INDIVIDUAL EXERCISE

Here is an exercise you can do by yourself that can help your heart and lungs stay healthy. Before starting, do some stretching exercises. Then do the exercise below hard enough to speed up your heartbeat and breathing. Keep exercising for at least 12 minutes after your heartbeat and breathing have speeded up. You can do more than one exercise as long as you do not stop to rest between exercises.

Jumping Jacks

1. Stand with your feet together. Put your arms at your sides.

2. Jump up, spread your feet apart, and swing your arms up. Land in the position shown in picture 5. Your feet should be a little further apart than the width of your shoulders.

3. Jump up again. As you jump, bring your feet together and your arms down. Land in the starting position.

4. Repeat steps 2 and 3 in an even rhythm ten times.

5

GROUP EXERCISE

Playing an active game with your friends is a good way to exercise. It is also fun. Here is an active game that you and your friends might have fun playing. Remember to stretch out well before you start playing any active game.

Swim Shark Swim

This is a running game that will exercise your heart and lungs. You can play this game with 10 or more people. You will need a playing area with two base lines. They should be between 60 and 90 feet (18.2 meters and 26.3 meters) apart.

6

1. The object of the game is to turn everyone into "sea sponges."

2. Choose two or three people to be "sea monsters," or "its." The sea monsters stand in the middle of the playing area as shown in picture 6. All the other players should be standing on one of the base lines. They are the "sharks."

3. To begin, the sea monsters call out "swim shark swim."

4. The sharks on the base line try to run to the other base line without getting tagged.

5. If a shark is tagged by a sea monster, the shark turns into a sea sponge. A sea sponge must stand where he or she is caught. Sea sponges can move their arms but not their feet.

6. Sea monsters return to the middle again. They face the sharks who have made it to the second base line. The sea monsters again call out "swim shark swim." The remaining sharks try to run back to the first base line without being tagged.

7. Running sharks can be tagged by sea sponges. Then these sharks become sea sponges, too.

8. Continue the game until all the sharks are caught. Then pick new sea monsters and start again.

COOLING DOWN

Always end your exercising with a few exercises that will allow your body to cool down slowly. You can use many of the same exercises for cooling down as for stretching out. For cooling down, you should do an exercise fewer times than for stretching out. You should also do the exercise more slowly. Here are some exercises you can use to cool down.

Lower Spine Stretch

1. Sit on the floor with your back straight. Bend your knees and put the soles of your feet together.

2. Make sure your toes are in line with your nose. Your feet should not touch your body. Your hips should sit evenly on the floor.

3. Bend forward slowly. Put your head as close to the floor as you can as shown in picture 7.

7

4. Breathe deeply in and out. Do this four times. Try to feel your spine getting longer.

5. Sit up slowly. Relax.

Forward and Backward Bends

1. Stand with your back to a wall. Put your arms at your sides. You should be about one foot (30 centimeters) from the wall. Breathe deeply.

2. Breathe out slowly while bending your knees and the rest of your body. You should end up in the position shown in picture 8.

8

3. Breathe in again slowly. As you breathe in, raise your body slowly back to the position in step 1.

4. Raise your arms above your head. Bend backward until your fingertips touch the wall as shown in picture 9. Then return to the position in step 1.

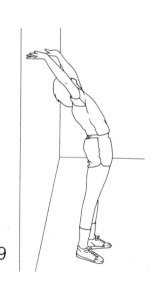

9

5. Complete steps 2 through 4 three times.

6. Finish by taking two deep breaths. Then relax. Let your body rest.

GLOSSARY

This glossary contains major health words and their definitions introduced in this text. A page number follows each definition. It tells where to find the word in the text.

Each glossary word is in **dark** type. The correct way to say each word is given in the special spelling in ( ) after that word. For example, the word <u>accident</u> appears this way: **ac·ci·dent** (ˈak-səd-ənt).

The sounds used in the spellings in ( ) are explained in the Pronunciation Key below. Each symbol or letter stands for a sound. You can recognize this sound in the words following it.

Most glossary words have the mark ˈ placed before a syllable. This mark shows you that the syllable is said with more force, or stress, than the other syllables in the word, as in the word **al·co·hol** (ˈal-kə-hȯl).

Pronunciation Key

a	cat, lap, bad	j	jet, germ, just	th	that, there
ā	say, late, take	k	keep, crawl	ü	rude, booth
ä	father, lot	l	pale	u̇	put, stood
au̇	cow, shout, mouth	m	man, him	v	river
b	bubble, bib	n	not, loan	w	wall, power
ch	chill	ŋ	linger, young	y	you, yellow
d	dot, do	ō	tone, hope	yü	fuel, mule
e	let, red	ȯ	law, tall	yu̇	pure
ē	meat, cheese	ȯi	join	z	gaze, rise
f	puff	p	cap	zh	decision
g	got, bag	r	bread, far	ə	(represents)
h	happy	s	soul, moss		a in amount
hw	white, where	sh	shut, ocean		e in thicken
i	lip, give	t	tap		i in edible
ī	bite, tie	th	tooth, within		o in cannon
					u in catsup

A

ac·ci·dent ('ak-səd-ənt), unexpected event that could harm someone. **170**

ac·ids ('as-ədz), chemicals that usually have a sour taste and can break down tooth enamel. **64**

act (akt), the way a person does something. **13**

ac·tions ('ak-shəns), things people do. **15**

air pol·lu·tion (ar pə-'lü-shən), dirt and other materials that are harmful to breathe. **204**

al·co·hol ('al-kə-hȯl), drug that is found in beer, wine, and liquor. **157**

al·ler·gy ('al-ər-jē), the body's unusual reaction to something. **133**

an·ti·bi·ot·ic (an-ti-bī-'ät-ik), drug made from certain living things. **149**

an·ti·bod·ies ('ant-i-bäd-ēz), things in the body that surround germs and stop the germs from getting what they need from cells. **127**

B

bac·te·ria (bak-'tir-ē-ə), one group of germs that needs food and water to live. **127**

bal·anced di·et ('bal-ənst 'di-ət), foods to be eaten every day that include food from each of the four food groups. **83**

blood ves·sels (bləd 'ves-əlz), tubes that carry blood around the body. **35**

boost·ers ('bü-stərs), immunizations given again. **136**

brain (brān), part of the body that is used to think and that tells the body when to move and to do other things. **37**

C

caf·feine (ka-'fēn), drug found in coffee, tea, cocoa, and some cola drinks. **157**

cal·is·then·ics (kal-əs-'then-iks), sets of exercises that a person can do regularly. **113**

cal·o·ries ('kal-ə-rēz), measure of how much energy food gives the body when the food is burned. **80**

car·ing ('ker-iŋ), helping other people feel good. **4**

cav·i·ties ('kav-ət-ēz), tooth decay. **64**

cells (selz), smallest living parts of the body. **34**

chapped (chapt), made rough and sore. **52**

choic·es (chois-əz), things that a person decides for himself or herself. **30**

com·mu·ni·ca·ble ill·ness·es (kə-'myü-ni-kə-bəl 'il-nəs-əz), illnesses that can be passed from one person to another. **128**

com·mu·ni·ty (kə-'myü-nət-ē), place where people live, work, play, and go to school. **194**

con·sid·er·a·tion (kən-sid-ə-'rā-shən), thinking about other people's feelings. **8**

co·op·er·a·tion (kō-äp-ə-'rā-shən), people helping one another in order to make things work well. **8**

D

den·tal floss ('dent-əl fläs), strong thread used to clean under the gums and between the teeth. **66**

den·tin ('dent-ən), layer under the enamel of a tooth. **64**

der·mis ('dər-məs), bottom layer of the skin. **52**

di·a·be·tes (dī-ə-'bēt-ēz), an illness in which a person's blood has too much sugar. **134**

di·et ('di-ət), what a person usually eats and drinks. **81**

di·ges·tion (dī-'jes-chən), the breaking up and changing of food by the body so the cells can use the food. **92**

dis·clos·ing tab·let (dis-'klōz-iŋ 'tab-lət), tablet with harmless red dye in it that shows where plaque is found on teeth. **62**

drugs (drəgz), things other than food that can make changes in the body. **148**

E

emer·gen·cy (i-'mər-jən-sē), sudden need that calls for immediate help. **176**

enam·el (in-'am-əl), hard, outer layer of a tooth. **62**

en·er·gy ('en-ər-jē), strength the body uses to do its work. **37**

epi·der·mis (ep-ə-'dər-məs), top layer of the skin. **52**

esoph·a·gus (i-'saf-ə-gəs), pipe in the body through which food reaches the stomach. **92**

ex·er·cise ('ek-sər-sīz), any activity that makes the body work hard. **100**

F

fam·i·ly ('fam-ə-lē), you and the people at home. **4**

fe·ver ('fē-vər), body temperature that is higher than normal. **126**

flu·o·ride ('flu-ər-īd), chemical that helps protect the teeth against tooth decay. **64**

food chain (füd chān), link among plants, animals, and people for food. **77**

G

germs (jərmz), tiny, living creatures that can be seen only through a microscope. **53**

goals (gōlz), things a person wants that he or she works to reach. **107**

H

hab·it ('hab-ət), something done often without thinking very much about it. **80**

haz·ards ('haz-ərdz), dangers. **170**

head lice (hed līs), tiny insects that can live on the scalp and make it itch. **55**

health work·ers (helth 'wər-kərz), persons who try to keep people healthy. **201**

heart (härt), thick, hollow muscle in the chest that pumps blood around the body. **35**

height (hīt), how tall a person is. **32**

I

im·mune (im-'yün), protected from an illness. **136**

im·mu·ni·za·tions (im-yə-nə-'zā-shənz), vaccines given by injection or swallowed. **136**

in·gre·di·ents (in-'grēd-ē-ənts), things that go into a food. **82**

L

large in·tes·tine (lärj in-'tes-tən), part of the body into which wastes from food go until they are ready to leave the body. **92**

lim·it ('lim-it), point at which a person must stop. **172**

lit·ter·ing ('lit-ər-iŋ), dropping trash on the ground. **206**

lung can·cer (ləng 'kan-sər), serious illness in which cells of the lungs grow out of control and form lumps. **160**

lungs (ləngz), parts of the body inside the chest that help a person breathe. **36**

M

med·i·cines ('med-ə-sənz), things that can help prevent illnesses or help make a person well when a person is ill. **136**

mi·cro·scope ('mī-krə-skōp), an instrument that makes very small things look bigger. **34**

mus·cles ('məs-əlz), groups of tissues that help the body move. **101**

mus·cle tone ('məs-əl tōn), firmness of muscles. **106**

226

N

nic·o·tine ('nik-ə-tēn), drug found in tobacco smoke that can damage a smoker's heart. **157**

noise pol·lu·tion (nòiz pə-'lü-shən), loud noises that can be harmful to a person's health. **207**

nu·cle·us ('nü-klē-əs), part of each cell that directs the activities of the cell. **34**

nu·tri·ents ('nü-trē-ənts), parts of food that help the body grow and give it energy. **79**

O

oil glands (òil glandz), parts of the body that send out oil made in the skin through tiny tubes. **52**

over-the-coun·ter med·i·cines ('ō-vər-thə-'kaùnt-ər med-ə-sənz), medicines that can be bought without a special order from a doctor; also called **OTC medicines.** **151**

ox·y·gen ('äk-si-jən), gas that the cells need and that is in the air a person breathes. **36**

P

pas·sen·ger ('pas-ən-jər), person who rides along with a driver. **181**

pe·des·tri·an (pə-'des-trē-ən), person who is walking. **184**

pen·i·cil·lin (pen-ə-'sil-ən), very strong antibiotic drug made from mold. **149**

per·ma·nent teeth ('pərm-ə-nənt tēth), second set of teeth. **29**

phar·ma·cist ('fär-mə-səst), person who prepares medicines by following a doctor's order. **151**

phys·i·cal ther·a·pists ('fiz-i-kəl 'ther-ə-pəsts), specially trained people who help find physical activities for people with special physical problems. **117**

phys·i·cal ther·a·py ('fiz-i-kəl 'ther-ə-pē), special exercises to help make a part of the body strong again. **117**

phys·i·cal trait ('fiz-i-kəl trāt), feature that tells something special about a person's body. **42**

plaque (plak), thin, sticky film of germs that forms on the hard, outer layer of teeth. **62**

pol·lute (pə-'lüt), to harm air and water by adding harmful materials to them. **203**

pores (pōrz), small openings in the skin through which sweat and oil leave the body. **52**

pre·scrip·tion (pri-'skrip-shən), doctor's order for a special medicine. **151**

pre·scrip·tion med·i·cines (pri-'skrip-shən 'med-ə-sənz), medicines that can be bought only with the order of a doctor. **152**

pri·ma·ry teeth ('prī-mer-ē tēth), first set of teeth. **29**

pulp (pəlp), inside part of a tooth below the dentin. **64**

R

re·cy·cling cen·ter (rē-'sī-klin 'sen-tər), place where cans, bottles, and newspapers can be made useful again. **208**

S

safe·ty rule ('saf-tē rül), rule that helps keep a person from harm. **170**

safe·ty work·ers ('saf-tē 'wər-kərz), people who try to keep other people safe. **197**

shar·ing ('sher-in), use of the same things by more than one person. **9**

side ef·fects (sīd i-'fekts), unneeded changes in the body that some drugs may cause. **156**

skel·e·ton ('skel-ət-ən), bones that help give the body its shape and help protect the inside of the body from harm. **101**

skills (skilz), things a person is able to do well. **29**

small in·tes·tine (smȯl in-'tes-tən), part of the body that receives food from the stomach. **92**

stom·ach ('stəm-ək), part of the body that squeezes and mashes food. **92**

sweat glands (swet 'glandz), parts of the body with tiny tubes that carry sweat out of the body. **52**

symp·toms ('simp-təmz), signs telling that something is wrong in the body. **126**

T

tar (tär), dark, sticky substance found in tobacco smoke. **157**

tis·sues ('tish-yüz), groups of the same kinds of cells that work together. **101**

trait (trāt), feature that tells something about a person. **42**

trust (trəst), feeling that people will always be there when they are needed. **27**

U

un·der·stand·ing (ən-dər-'stand-iŋ), knowing what someone else is feeling. **10**

V

vac·cine (vak-'sēn), medicine in immunizations that puts germs of a certain kind into the body. **136**

vi·rus ('vī-rəs), very tiny germ that kills living cells in order to live. **127**

vol·un·teer (väl-ən-'tir), person who works without pay. **202**

W

wastes (wāsts), parts of food that the body cannot use. **92**

wa·ter pol·lu·tion ('wȯt-ər pə-'lü-shən), harmful material in rivers, lakes, and oceans. **203**

weight (wāt), how heavy a person is. **26**

white blood cells (hwīt bləd selz), certain cells in the blood that help fight harmful germs when they get into the body. **127**

INDEX